SUSTAINABILITY AND THE CIVIL COMMONS:
RURAL COMMUNITIES IN THE AGE OF GLOBALIZATION

Often used but little understood, the word 'sustainability' is potent in its ability to evoke a better world based on economic, social, and environmental justice. In *Sustainability and the Civil Commons*, Jennifer Sumner explains why current definitions of sustainability are inadequate and offers a framework for a new understanding of sustainability centered on the civil commons, which includes such institutions and practices as universal health care, environmental treaties, workplace safety regulations, and public education.

The concept of sustainability has in fact been remarkably under-theorized. This work provides both a theoretical basis for sustainability and an image of a future that involves increased individual and community well-being grounded in environmental security. Using rural communities as her reference point, Sumner examines sustainability in the context of corporate globalization. She argues that globalizing the civil commons, not corporate-sponsored trade agreements, will open the way to true sustainability. Drawing on Antonio Gramsci's model of counter-hegemony, Jürgen Habermas's theory of communicative action, and John McMurtry's concept of life-value ethics, the author builds an original theoretical framework that combines global reach with local focus. Challenging and wide-ranging in scope, *Sustainability and the Civil Commons* will be an invaluable resource for scholars and practitioners interested in public policy, community development, and rural studies.

JENNIFER SUMNER is an assistant professor in the Adult Education and Community Development Program at the Ontario Institute for Studies in Education of the University of Toronto.

Sustainability and the Civil Commons

Rural Communities in the Age of Globalization

Jennifer Sumner

UNIVERSITY OF TORONTO PRESS
Toronto Buffalo London

© University of Toronto Press Incorporated 2005
Toronto Buffalo London
Printed in Canada

Reprinted in paperback 2007

ISBN 978-0-8020-7999-2 (cloth)
ISBN 978-0-8020-9527-5 (paper)

∞

Printed on acid-free paper

Library and Archives Canada Cataloguing in Publication

Sumner, Jennifer, 1949–
    Sustainability and the civil commons : rural communities in the
    age of globalization / Jennifer Sumner.

    Includes bibliographical references and index.
    ISBN 978-0-8020-7999-2 (bound). – ISBN 978-0-8020-9527-5 (pbk.)

    1. Sustainable development.   2. Globalization.   3. Capitalism.
    4. Cooperation.   5. Quality of life.   6. Canada – Rural conditions.
    I. Title.

    HC120.E5S86 2004   320.5′8   C2004-905650-6

University of Toronto Press acknowledges the financial assistance to
its publishing program of the Canada Council for the Arts and the
Ontario Arts Council.

University of Toronto Press acknowledges the financial support for
its publishing activities of the Government of Canada through the
Book Publishing Industry Development Program (BPIDP).

For my grandchildren – may they live in a more sustainable world

Contents

Acknowledgments

This book has been a labour of exhilaration, frustration, perseverance, and love. A number of people contributed to smoothing my path, and deserve recognition. I wish to thank friends and colleagues at the University of Guelph who helped along the way: Al Lauzon, Don Reid, Bob Brown, Heather Mair, and Wendy Milne. Thanks as well to Virgil Duff at the University of Toronto Press for his seasoned guidance, and to the anonymous reviewers of this book for their thoughtful insights and challenging suggestions.

I also want to thank my family for supporting this work, especially my partner, John, for his example of scholarship that makes a difference, and my son, JJ, who was always there when I needed advice. The birth of my grandchildren has encouraged me to take the long view and to consider the possibility of a better world than the one we currently inhabit, and I thank them for inspiring me.

And, finally, I wish to thank the people who have built the civil commons over millennia – your work has enabled all our lives to be more fufilled, more inclusive, and more sustainable.

SUSTAINABILITY AND THE CIVIL COMMONS

Introduction

> When basic threats to survival and well-being loom large, mere adjustments to the present path seem unlikely to be sufficient. What is needed instead is an attempt to imagine different, more desirable futures, and to see what they would be like and how they could be attained.[1]

Logging and land conversion to accommodate human demand have shrunk the world's forests by half and are now proceeding at over 130,000 square kilometres per year. More than 300 million people live on less than a dollar a day and that number is set to rise to 420 million over the next fifteen years. Three hundred of the world's transnational corporations together constitute a quarter of the world's productive assets, a number of them larger in wealth than the majority of nation states.[2]

With statistics like these, it is little wonder that *sustainability* has become an issue of immense importance around the world. Governments, non-governmental organizations (NGOs), corporations, municipalities, universities, citizens' groups, and supranational institutions are all becoming familiar with the term, invoking it to show their concern for the future. Yet, another term is invoked even more frequently: *globalization.* Yet, again to show their concern for the future, but for different reasons. Inspiring to some and terrifying to others, globalization affects people around the world, in developed and developing countries, in democracies and dictatorships, in urban and rural areas.

Both sustainability and globalization are crucial to the future of rural communities in Canada.[3] Value-laden and contested, these terms exist in a tension that plays out across the country. To a large extent, sustainability and globalization not only form the context within which daily life in rural communities takes place, but also pose the problems and drive the decisions made in these communities.

Rural communities are particularly vulnerable at the beginning of the twenty-first century. Their low population densities, spatial isolation, increasing lack of diversity, and persistent levels of poverty restrict the range and depth of choices that are available to their urban counterparts. In the face of these vulnerabilities, rural communities remain, however, a vital link between society and the natural environment. This link highlights the importance of their survival, and makes them crucial to the study of sustainability.

And yet, by some people's standards, rural communities are almost by definition unsustainable. In a newspaper article entitled 'Coast-to-Coast Subsidies Trap Rural Canada,' Lawrence Solomon has argued that the lifestyles of rural and small-town residents are unsustainable.[4] While ignoring the issue of the high-consumption lifestyles of many urban dwellers, he goes on to decry the provision of such life-sustaining services as water, telephone, electricity, natural gas, cable, and postal delivery to rural areas. As executive director of the Urban Renaissance Institute, Solomon claims that government policies ensuring these services have turned rural areas into welfare dependencies. He concludes, among other suggestions, that governments can finish the task of reviving rural areas by 'allowing the rural and small town populations to find their natural level.'

Implicit in Solomon's argument is an understanding of sustainability that is based on a system of values that promotes money first and foremost. This neoliberal take on sustainability equates it with adaptation to the demands of the global economy, leaving governments powerless to protect rural communities. Legislative attempts to ensure social safety nets, such as reducing the comparative costs of living in rural areas, are anathema to this value system and denounced as 'barriers to trade.' From a neoliberal perspective, the corporate quarterly report becomes the line in the sand that cannot be crossed without unsustainable repercussions. And with a neo-Darwinian twist of the knife, if rural communities do not adapt to the 'inevitability' of the global economy, they are not fit to survive.

But another perspective is on the rise, based on a different system of values. These values can be summarized as *life values* – values that promote life first and foremost. Philosopher John McMurtry contends that two master principles of *value-gain*, which he calls 'codes of value,' underlie the long economic war expressed by history.[5] While these codes of value have often been confused, he argues that the future of civil and planetary 'life-organization' depends on their distinction, especially given the present period of unregulated globalization. McMurtry calls these codes of value the 'money code of value' and the 'life code of value.' While the former has become the dominant, presupposed basis for more and more decisions affecting human and planetary life, the latter is (re)asserting itself as the vital underlying ground of existence. And it is life values that must ultimately guide any discussions of sustainability. Leaving sustainability to those who hold money values will result only in more of the degradation so often associated with the age of globalization.

As the world becomes increasingly interconnected through mechanisms like trade agreements and telecommunications, we are repeatedly told that the current form of globalization is inevitable, and that we must simply adjust to it. The adamance of those who hold this position is encapsulated in the TINA syndrome – an acronym for Margaret Thatcher's phrase, 'There is no alternative.' Such determinism seems to leave little choice for alternative ways of understanding the world, especially when it is tied to neoliberal assumptions that human beings are driven relentlessly by permanent and insatiable wants. But alternatives to the status quo enjoy a long history in human thought, and have often been formalized into visions that have been labelled as 'utopian.'

Utopia has been defined as an ideal commonwealth whose inhabitants exist under seemingly perfect conditions.[6] The term originated as the name of an imaginary island depicted by Sir Thomas More in 1516 in his book entitled *Utopia*, a Greek word meaning 'no place.' Since then, numerous other publications have set out their version of Utopia, from early visions of religious communities to a stream of new left utopias in the 1950s and 1960s, and the ecological utopias or 'ecotopias' that gave rise to the environmental movement of the 1970s and 1980s.[7]

Over time, the meaning of the term Utopia changed, taking on a negative aspect that sought to invalidate its original intent. While still associated with ideal commonwealths, it took on the notion of impossibility or unattainability. This negative connotation arose because utopian authors used their books as vehicles of criticism of their own societies, which made the term a target for invalidation.

In spite of such negative associations, the utopian project has endured. For almost 500 years, utopian writings have inspired human thought and action. As the choices in the twenty-first century seem to narrow to impossibly econometric ones that threaten both human existence and the natural environment of which we are a part, the need for utopian alternatives grows – alternatives that offer a vision that can be both inspirational *and* practical. Such visions are important not only because of their inspirational power, but also because of their ability to promote realistic change.

In Barry Carr's article, 'Globalization from Below,' in the *International Social Science Journal*, the author states: 'In the light of the ongoing destruction of the very foundation of our existence, the erosion of internal and external resources, to ask questions against the grain, and to engage in Utopian thinking becomes a matter of the most serious and conscientious realism.'[8]

This book will ask questions against the grain and engage in a kind of utopian thinking that will develop an alternative to what has been described as the 'steamroller' of globalization.[9] In the absence of alternatives, the so-called inevitability of the current form of globalization can turn into self-fulfilling prophecy. Envisioning an alternative is at the heart of this book. Such a vision speaks to what it means to be more fully human as opposed to what it means to be a consumer in the global market. This vision has a long history, which is captured in Oscar Wilde's observation that a map of the world which does not include Utopia is not even worth glancing at, for it leaves out the one country at which humanity is always arriving.[10]

This book will map out a country where human potential, not profit maximization, can be more fully realized. It will ask questions that challenge the steamroller of the single option that crushes this potential, and provide a serious alternative to open the way for its realization. This alternative will involve a new understanding of sustainability, one that has the vision and the operationalizability to be of service to rural communities.

Why are rural communities even worth preserving in this fast-changing world? In the web of Canadian life, rural communities are an integral component – a link to the past and a hope for the future. For a myriad of reasons, many people dream of rural life as an alternative to the troubles they face today, and that dream is worth keeping alive, in spite of its shortcomings.[11] In addition, the wealth of knowledge, range of skills, and diversity of people that make up our rural communities are a heritage and a way of life that should not be lost through our failure to understand the nature and challenge of their sustainability.

If rural communities are worth preserving, how can we ensure their future? The media and the academic literature are full of the struggles of rural communities, especially in the age of globalization. Restructuring, downsizing, privatization, deregulation, migration, unemployment, poverty, and insecurity are all taking their toll on rural communities, many of which are marginal to begin with. Yet a profound normative issue is seldom confronted. Rural communities should not survive just because they have learned to adapt to the demands of the global market. They should survive, and thrive, because they are home to many people, places of employment, centres of learning, and hives of biodiversity. In addition, they are the direct interface between humans and the natural environment. Rural communities add value, *in the life sense of the term*, to our lives and our experience. Without the farming villages, logging communities, mining towns, fishing hamlets, and remote settlements, what would remain of the human/nature interface beyond urban wasteland, agro-business monocultures, dumping grounds, industrial parks, clearcuts, and, at best, seasonal tourist attractions for capricious urban visitors?

The struggles of rural communities are well documented. Like rail service and public education, rural communities could become a casualty of the so-called 'efficiency' of globalization, an efficiency that serves money values but not life values. That is why the issue of sustainability is so important, and why it needs to be given a new orientation that centres on life values.

Where will the search for sustainability take us? The goal of sustainability is increased well-being, which is defined by the *Oxford English Dictionary* as 'the state of being or doing well in life; happy, healthy, or prosperous condition; moral or physical welfare (of a person or community).'[12] Fromm expanded on this understanding when he proposed that well-being means to be fully born, to become what one potentially is.[13] This meaning of well-being speaks to the realization of human potential that is at the heart of the utopian project. In this way, well-being is not only the goal of sustainability, but also the portal to the realization of that potential. It is the connection between the concrete world that is and the utopian world that could be.

Wolfgang Sachs begins to make the linkage between sustainability, well-being, and the utopian project when he asserts that sustainability in the last instance springs from a fresh inquiry into the meaning of the good life.[14] Prugh, Costanza, and Daly make the linkage directly when they maintain that 'the unifying theme of utopian visions throughout history is how to provide for the common good in a world made unfair and unpredictable by both nature and human flaws. Utopian writings and experiments explore ways to arrange society to do a better job of promoting well-being. That is also the aim of the quest to achieve sustainability.'[15]

If the goal of sustainability is increased well-being, why haven't we reached it yet? Why is sustainability under siege and well-being in retreat? In his book entitled *Sustainers and Sustainabililty*, Doob quotes the German editor of a volume on nature and discusses his comments: '"Why really are we not living in Paradise? ... For this are we too stupid, too unfit, too wicked, or all of these?" It is almost impossible to comprehend sustainability without raising similar questions and hence referring to individuals who are or are not sustaining or being sustained now or in the future.'[16]

While we all might indeed wonder why we are not living in Paradise, we shouldn't be looking to our own shortcomings for the answer, but to the context in which we are increasingly forced to operate. Exemplified by Solomon's dismissal of rural communities, that context is the money values of neoclassical economics and its globalization agenda: 'Conventional (neoclassical) economics is the reigning economic world-view of our time. Its assumptions are taught in every basic college economics course and reflected in every economics story in the newspaper. Its precepts guide the relations of governments with business and with each other. They are so pervasive as to be almost undetectable, like water is to a fish.'[17]

Both sustainability and well-being are under assault, marginalized by a globalization agenda that sees them as externalities in the race to increase market share and profits. That race has few winners, but many losers – those who experience the now-famous 'race to the bottom.' Such peripheralization is a by-product of this agenda, another externality that does not register with those who pursue it. As the ranks of the excluded increase, the only well-being that counts is the well-being of quarterly corporate profits. In this money-values context, rural communities face powerful challenges to their sustainability.

Understanding sustainability is very similar to the problem of understanding life itself.[18] It is just as serious and just as difficult. This book will examine the concept of sustainability in the context of rural communities, develop a new understanding of sustainability and argue that sustainability can result in increased individual and community well-being. It will also examine the concept of globalization and argue that some forms of globalization can interrupt, reduce and even destroy sustainability, result in decreased well-being for individuals and communities, and ultimately ruin the natural environment on which we depend for our existence.

Chapter 1 sets the context of the search for sustainability by looking at the age of globalization from both a money-values and a life-values perspective. It traces the history of the concept from its roots in the ideas of the global village and global society to its growing acceptance around the world. This growing acceptance is not necessarily a positive development. According to Gordon Laxer, 'one of the main effects of globalization talk, in its popular discourse guise, has been to break down resistance to the entry of foreign transnational corporations and banks.'[19] To combat this breakdown, it is important to ask just what is being globalized: are corporate rights, the unrestricted flow of capital and the unregulated movement of goods being globalized or are human rights, environmental protection, the free movement of labour, and universal public health care and education being globalized? From this perspective, the answer is clear – the former are being promoted at the expense of the latter.

These very different sets of parameters represent two manifestations of globalization that have important ramifications in the search for sustainability: *corporate globalization* (also known as economic globalization, neoliberal globalization, or globalization from above) and *globalization from below*, which brings many forms of resistance to corporate globalization under its collective rubric. Corporate globalization is based on the money code of value – that is, it operates out of a system of values that puts money first and foremost, no matter what. The proponents of this globalization from above

> promised that it would benefit all: that it would 'raise all boats.' Workers and communities around the globe were told that if they downsized, deregulated, eliminated social services, and generally became more competitive, the benefits of globalization would bless them. The poorest and most desperate were promised that they would see their standard of living increase if they accepted neoliberal austerity measures. They kept their end of the bargain, but globalization from above did not reciprocate. Instead, it is aggravating old and creating new problems for people and the environment.[20]

The problems that are either aggravated or created by corporate globalization are clearly evident in the 2003 United Nations' *Human Development Report 2003.*[21] It found that fifty-four countries saw the average income decline during the 1990s, and that twenty-one countries went backwards in terms of human development, which is a measure of income, life expectancy, and literacy. This reverse development is no accident, but the predictable outcome of a system of money values that always trumps life values in the endless search for increased profits. But the life-destroying outcomes of corporate globalization have provoked a worldwide movement of resistance: globalization from below. Based on the life code of value, globalization from below is a means by which 'people at the grassroots around the world link up to impose their own needs and interests on the process of globalization.'[22] Never before has so much local resistance been able to make so many global connections to challenge what has come to be understood as a common enemy. As members of an emerging social movement who operate out of a life-values perspective, those who see themselves as part of globalization from below are networking with their counterparts in other movements and countries, questioning the power of transnational corporations, developing a shared vision, constructing a common movement, and building solidarity. Now a permanent feature in the global landscape, globalization from below is 'rooted in a deep social reality: the need to control the forces of global capital.'[23] While globalization from below has its limitations,[24] it is a dynamic phenomenon that has helped to expose the darker sides of globalization.

These darker sides become frighteningly apparent when we focus on rural communities in the age of globalization. The impacts of corporate globalization are similar for both rural and urban communities, but unlike urban communities, rural communities lack the resources for dealing with these impacts. Chapter 2, summarizing an interdisciplinary range of studies in rural communities over a twenty-year period, traces the economic, political, social, environmental, gendered, and cultural impacts of corporate globalization on rural communities and concludes that corporate globalization has had devastating effects on rural communities both in Canada and around the world.

Given these unrelenting impacts, Chapter 3 begins the search for sustainability by building a theory for practice. Using the concepts of hegemony from Antonio Gramsci, communicative action from Jürgen Habermas, and the life code of value and the money code of value from John McMurtry, it outlines a theoretical model for engaging with the problems and possibilities of sustainability. The model can be a tool for analysis by offering a way of assessing the effectiveness of current under-standings of sustainability, and it can be a tool for construction by providing the basic building blocks for a new understanding of sustainability: counter-hegemony, dialogue, and life values. As a central strategy in the search for sustainability, this model forms the foundation of a working alternative to the relentless drive for capital accumulation that characterizes corporate globalization.

Chapter 4 examines the concept of sustainability, beginning with its origins in the English language in the early 1970s. Mired in controversy, the problems surrounding sustainability begin with the idea itself. The literature contains many contradictory interpretations of this elusive word. While some see it as a goal, objective, or end state, others see it as a state, condition, or characteristic. Some see it as a vision, an ethic, a principle, or a metabelief, and others as tantamount to a religion. Some reduce it to a management practice, while others dress it up as a manifestation of the second law of thermodynamics. Some associate sustainability with systems thinking and others see it as a form of mediation. And some consider it a social construct, while others argue that sustainability is a process.

An examination of the history of the concept of sustainability reveals controversy about its first use in the English language. While one source claims it was initially used in a publication by an economist, another argues that it was inaugurated at a United Nations conference. Regardless of the disagreements about its first usage, however, there is widespread agreement that the watershed in the history of sustainability was definitely the Brundtland Report, published in 1987 by the World Commission on Environment and Development (WCED), under the title *Our Common Future*. Increased acceptance reflected in the growing popularity of the term became a two-edged sword as transnational corporations began to co-opt sustainability as window dressing in their propaganda offensive against criticisms of the destructive impacts of corporate globalization. The definitions of sustainability put forward were conveniently vague and predictably varied, leading to confusion and increasing the controversy surrounding the term. This is where the analytical power of the theoretical model comes into play. Looking through the lens of the model, current definitions of sustainability are examined for their ability to deal with the devastating impacts of corporate globalization on rural communities and found wanting. And yet, these unrelenting impacts demand that we find an understanding of sustainability that provides a practical vision of a life that does not centre on serving capital accumulation for transnational corporations.

Chapter 5 – the heart of the book – proposes this new vision of sustainability, one we have been engaging with for millennia, but below the level of consciousness. Based in the building blocks of the theoretical model – counter-hegemony, dialogue and life values – it links sustainability to the concept of the *civil commons* in order to promote increased individual and community well-being in the age of globalization. The concept of the civil commons was developed by John McMurtry to describe 'any co-operative human construct that enables the access of all members of a community to life goods.' Based in life values, the civil commons is co-operative, not competitive, in its engagement with the world. It is a human construct, not a naturally occurring phenomenon, and must be built by human agency. It enables access for all community members, not just a privileged elite, so everyone has the chance to 'grow and express themselves as human,' and this community can range from the local through the national to the global community. And it provides 'life goods,' or means of life, which are whatever allows life to be preserved or extended on the three planes of being: organic movement, sensation, and feeling, and conceptual and image thought. These life goods that the civil commons provides range from nutritious food, clean water, and adequate shelter to education, health care, open spaces, and a safe workplace. In opposition to the money values of corporate globalization, 'not one civil commons institution or practice is instituted or financed to generate money profit for private investors. All are publicly formed over time to protect and enhance the lives of community members as a value in itself.'[25]

Examples of the civil commons surround us every day: public education, universal health care, parks, environmental legislation, health and safety regulations, and public broadcasting. In rural communities it takes the form of rural schools and post offices, farmers' co-operatives, marketing boards, and barn raisings. In spite of its constant presence, the civil commons has remained not only unnamed, but also 'unrecognized and untheorized as the unifying infrastructure of every successful social order throughout history.' This lack of awareness is what allows the life goods of the civil commons to be stripped away by transnational corporations and sold back at a profit to those of us who are in a position to pay for them. The increasing numbers of people who cannot afford them are left to struggle on their own and are blamed for their misfortunes. As externalities in the global race for capital accumulation, these people are unable to grow and express themselves as fully human. This is why the civil commons is central to sustainability and to the utopian project. It opens the door to increased well-being and the realization of human potential for more than just the privileged few. It links the concrete world of co-operative acts of human agency to the utopian dream of a better life for all that we catch glimpses of in, for example, universal health care. In sum: 'The organizing idea of the civil commons integrates all of society's protection and provision of unpriced life goods into a common supporting structure of social meaning shared by all cultures. The civil commons is, we might say, the long-missing link between the *is* of economic organization for ever-accumulating private-profit maximization, on the one hand, and the *ought* of social organization for citizens' vital life-needs and capacities, on the other.'[26]

With sustainability firmly tied to the civil commons, Chapter 6 sketches the outlines of future research based on a new understanding of sustainability. Using the compound terms *sustainable development* and *sustainable rural community*, it explores what they could become if given the life-values orientation of the civil commons. From this perspective, sustainable development would involve the development of the civil commons, not business development. Sustainable rural communities would involve building the civil commons in rural communities, not stripping it away as some kind of unsustainable lifestyle or 'welfare dependency.' Chapter 6 also introduces a new concept, sustainable globalization, as a life-values alternative to the money-values orientation of corporate globalization. Instead of trade agreements, capital flows, and product movement being globalized, the civil commons would be globalized – unearthed from its infinite but unconscious daily practices of care and inclusion to become the centrepiece of a truly sustainable world.

In the age of globalization, there can be no greater need than understanding sustainability, and rural communities provide the perfect reference point for meeting this need. They are the canary in the mine that warns us of impending disaster, the feedback loop that tells us all is not well. The sustainability of our rural communities is, in the end, a reflection of our overall sustainability. We can actively choose our sustainability by following a life-values perspective or we can passively leave it to the money values of those who dominate the global economy. Choosing our sustainability is not as difficult as might be imagined. We have actually been doing it for thousands of years, but below the level of consciousness. This book reaches down to the shared ground of our existence and reveals sustainability to be a very human, and very Canadian, way of life.

1 The Age of Globalization

Philosophers may rejoice: Finally a Word seems to have become the World.[1]

Both sustainability and rural communities could be added to the endangered species list – victims of global forces that become stronger every day. Sustainability suffers from vagueness, overuse, and co-option, while rural communities struggle under the impacts of worldwide changes such as restructuring and migration. We are living in an era when money values dictate that many people and the communities they live in are increasingly dispensable, while at the same time life values bring people and communities together through a shared ground of mutual commitment. Welcome to the age of globalization.

This chapter will investigate the meaning of globalization, tracing the history of the term from its obscure beginnings to its current dominant status. It will concentrate on two manifestations of globalization that directly affect sustainability: corporate globalization and globalization from below. Based in opposing systems of value, these forms of globalization play a major role in the search for sustainability.

What has been called the 'horrible neologism' of globalization has its origins in two different disciplines: in communication sciences with Marshall McLuhan's concept of the global village; and in strategic studies with Zbigniew Brzezinski's proclamation of the birth of a global society – the American one – capable of making its way of life universal because of its economic primacy and the dominance of new technologies.[2] A fairly new term in the English language, *globalization* was first used in 1959 in the *Economist* to refer to quotas of car imports. Although a prescient 1962 article in the *Spectator* referred to it as 'a staggering concept,' no one at that time could have fathomed the global and local effects that it would engender.[3]

Therborn reports that acceptance of the term was slow. The *Social Science Citation Index* records only a small number of occurrences of the term in the 1980s, but shows its soaring popularity from 1992 onwards, a popularity that accelerated in the last years of the past century. It was not listed in the major dictionaries of English, French, Spanish, and German in the 1980s or the first half of the 1990s. In Arabic, at least four different words render the notion of globalization; in Japanese business, the word goes back to the 1980s; in China, it only entered academic language in the mid-1990s. The Thai Royal Academy has translated globalization as *lokapiwat*, meaning expanding globally or conquering the world.[4]

While some see just one form of globalization, others see multiple manifestations. For example, Meyer sees five dimensions: increased political and military interdependence, increased economic interdependencies, an expanded flow of individual persons, expanded interdependence of expressive culture, and expanded flow in instrumental culture. Therborn talks in the plural of globalizations, mentioning five major topical discourses: competition economics, sociocritical, state (im)potence, culture, and planetary ecology.[5]

To add to the complexity of the topic, some see globalization as a recent phenomenon, while others give it an historical trajectory. Therborn sees six waves of globalization: the diffusion of world religions and the establishment of transcontinental civilizations; European colonial conquests in naval operations; a global thrust resulting from purely intra-European power struggles; European imperialism; the politico-military dynamic of the Cold War; and the current, mainly financial-cum-cultural dynamic. On the other hand, Shiva sees only three historical waves of globalization: European colonialism, the imposition of Western development, and the current era of free trade.[6]

This longer view of the globalization process is an important consideration, especially for a country like Canada that has an abundance of natural resources, or staples, and a reliance on export. As a product of European colonialism, according to political economist Mel Watkins, Canada is long familiar with the foreign-controlled, global trading networks that characterize current understandings of globalization. His views echo those of historian J.M.S. Careless: 'Canada took shape through the successive occupation of frontiers, the forward margins of an acquisitive society reaching out to fresh areas of resources. When sixteenth-century Europe advanced a fishing frontier to the northeastern coasts of

North America, a process began which eventually brought the whole Canadian land mass and its indigenous peoples into recorded history.'[7] Careless saw this process as ongoing, with successive waves of European migrants and their descendants invading one great resource region after another, with frontiers of fishing, fur trading, lumbering, farming, ranching, or mining. He described how these frontiers were seen as more than moving margins of pioneer farm seekers – they were understood as expanding supply zones for civilization.[8]

While initially a positive form of development for Canada, over time this process came to hold dangers for the country. As Harold Innis argued, we stood 'on the one hand in danger of being burned at the stake of natural resources and on the other hand of being boiled in the oil of unrestricted competition.' And in a prescient overview, Careless emphasized that 'the metropolitan-hinterland relationship can be found all around the world and ... its global embrace may show many international aspects or, in more recent times, the spreading activities of multinational corporations ... Is the modern multinational, in its high dealings with states and potentates, perhaps the old English East India Company writ large? No – I think not: the East India Company probably showed more responsibility.'[9]

Canada's long relationship with foreign-controlled global trading networks continues today in the guise of the North American Free Trade Agreement (NAFTA). 'Sold as an industrial strategy that would make Canadian manufacturing efficient, it may well be entrenching the staples status of the Canadian economy.'[10]

While the globalization process has a long trajectory, most agree, however, that we are currently deep in the age of globalization, and that its consequences are far-reaching. One exception to this majority consensus is Immanuel Wallerstein, who argues that we are not in the age of globalization, but in the 'age of transition.' For Wallerstein, globalization has existed for about 500 years, a time frame he calls the life cycle of the capitalist 'world-economy,' 'which had its period of genesis, its period of normal development and now has entered into its period of terminal crisis.' Within this 500-year time frame is another, shorter time frame, which runs from 1945 to today. This cyclical rhythm is what Wallerstein describes as 'a typical Kondratieff cycle of the capitalist world-economy,' one that has two parts: an upward swing or economic expansion that went from 1945 to 1967–73, and a downward swing or economic contraction that has been going from 1967–73 to today, and 'probably will continue on for several more years.' We are now in what

Wallerstein calls the age of transition, an age in which 'the world-system is finding itself in acute moral and institutional crisis' and will be transformed into something else.[11]

While geographer David Harvey agrees that we are in transition, this does not mean that globalization is finished or that the entire capitalist world-system will be transformed into something else. Harvey sees globalization not 'as an undifferentiated unity but as a geographically articulated patterning of global capitalist activities and relations.' For Harvey, 'capitalism is a constantly revolutionary force in world history, a force that perpetually re-shapes the world into new and often quite unexpected configurations.' One well-known configuration of capitalism is Fordism, understood by Harvey as a full-fledged and distinctive regime of accumulation that has to be seen less as a mere system of mass production and more as a total way of life. The Fordist regime held firm at least until 1973, when the sharp recession of that year began a process of rapid, and as yet not well understood, transition in the regime of accumulation.[12]

For Harvey, the crisis in Fordism 'was simply that the mechanisms evolved for controlling crisis tendencies were finally overwhelmed by the power of the underlying contradictions of capitalism.' To deal with these contradictions, some other and superior regime of capitalist production had to be created which would assure a solid basis for further accumulation on a global scale. That regime, or new configuration of capitalism, Harvey calls flexible accumulation, which rests on flexibility with respect to labour processes, labour markets, products, and patterns of consumption. Turnover time in production, always one of the keys to capitalist profitability, is reduced dramatically under a regime of flexible accumulation, but this accelerated turnover time would be useless unless the turnover time in consumption was also reduced. According to Harvey: 'Flexible accumulation has been accompanied on the consumption side, therefore, by a much greater attention to quick-changing fashions and the mobilization of all the artifices of need inducement and cultural transformation that this implies. The relatively stable aesthetic of Fordist modernism has given way to all the ferment, instability, and fleeting qualities of a postmodernist aesthetic that celebrates difference, ephemerality, spectacle, fashion, and the commodification of cultural forms.'[13] While Harvey sees much that is 'refreshing' about postmodernism, he argues that there is nothing about postmodernism in general that inhibits the further development of capital accumulation: 'Capital accumulation has always been about speed-up.'[14]

Overall, Harvey argues, it is important to emphasize to what degree flexible accumulation has to be seen as a particular and perhaps new combination of mainly old elements within the overall logic of capital accumulation. While he argues that there has been a sea change in cultural as well as in political-economic practices – the rise of post-modernist cultural forms, the emergence of more flexible modes of capital accumulation, and a new round of 'time-space compression' in the organization of capitalism – these changes 'appear more as shifts in surface appearance rather than as signs of the emergence of some entirely new postcapitalist or even postindustrial society.'[15]

It is clear, then, that globalization is a deeply complex term, implying a kind of worldwide connectedness while hiding an accumulation agenda that favours transnational corporations. Like a mantra or a catechism, it is endlessly repeated without a clear understanding of what it means. Seen by some as 'the process whereby the population of the world is increasingly bonded into a single society,' globalization has also been described as a 'world system in which powerful, interconnected, stateless corporations nullify national boundaries and incorporate whole societies as cost-effective sites of production.'[16]

Two important manifestations of globalization directly affect the sustainability of human and planetary life: corporate globalization (sometimes referred to as economic globalization or 'globalization from above'), and, in response, 'globalization from below,' which involves grassroots resistance to corporate globalization. Each manifestation instantiates and promotes an opposing set of values: corporate globalization is based on and perpetuates money values, while globalization from below is based on and perpetuates life values. In essence, living in the age of globalization means that we are embroiled in a 'war of values.'[17] This is the context in which the search for sustainability must be carried out.

Within this war of values, money values are currently in ascendance, exemplified by the increasingly frenzied drive for capital accumulation, regardless of the social or environmental consequences. Their imposition is now being 'systematized' through the rules developed in global trade rounds, and enforced by the World Trade Organization. These rules not only avoid responsibility for the impact of disruptive policies on workers and the environment, they also 'frustrate national and local efforts to legislate and live by deeply rooted social values.'[18]

Ultimately, the kind of pan-corporatism entailed by the money values of corporate globalization worries many people because of the lack of attention to human and environmental needs, the ease with which it downloads risk to those least able to bear it, and the toleration of grotesque disparities in wealth. In Canada, the moderator of the United Church warned that people were getting chewed up by an uncaring economy: 'People are dying in the process ... they are being sacrificed, literally, to the god of the market.' The World Council of Churches, in condemning 'unlimited economic growth and a continuous and un-regulated expansion of production and consumption for the world's rich,' appealed through the United Nations Commission on Sustainable Development for 'governments, international institutions and people of good will to demonstrate moral courage and political will to confront the excesses of globalization.'[19]

The value implications of corporate globalization are often pushed outside the realm of consideration, but must be challenged if rural communities are to survive the age of globalization. In essence, there are fundamental ethical questions about the sustainability of a global structure that perpetuates high degrees of international inequality while working with rural communities with little chance of satisfying even the most basic of their needs.[20]

To satisfy those needs, we require a value reorientation – a new way of looking at the world, one that places the flourishing of life ahead of the accumulation of money. We must counter the ascendance of money values with the affirmation of life values, which promote life first and foremost. To begin this reorientation, we need to look more closely at corporate globalization, and at the resistance that is building against it.

Corporate Globalization

Corporate globalization is known by a number of names. Some refer to it as globalization, economic globalization, or financial globalization; others label it mature capitalism, imperialism, colonialism, or globalization from above. Those who support corporate globalization hold a different set of values than those who oppose it. Working from a money-values perspective, the advocates of corporate globalization argue that it will build 'an inclusive world economy,' 'spread the wealth,' and result in 'large potential gains.' These gains are not only 'the profits of western and third-world corporations but productive employment and higher incomes for the world's poor.'[21]

Within the field of economics, corporate globalization is understood as the process by which the perceived advantages of Western-style capitalism have been shared with an ever-widening group of developing countries. Associated with the 'dismantling of national barriers to the operation of capital markets which began in the early 1980s,' corporate globalization is seen by economists as 'the means for harnessing humanity's basest instincts through appropriate institutional design to produce public good.'[22]

In order to further the public good, the advocates of corporate globalization have joined with the United Nations to expedite globalization. The International Chamber of Commerce (ICC) and the United Nations have committed themselves to 'forge a close global partnership to secure greater business input into the world's economic decision-making and boost the private sector in the least developed countries.'[23] When describing this partnership, the secretary general of the ICC, Maria Livanos Cattaui, reported that 'What makes the dialogue possible is the perception by both sides that open markets are a precondition for spreading more widely the benefits of globalization, and for integrating developing countries into the world economy.'[24]

Armed with the support of the United Nations, the president of the ICC, Helmut Maucher, declared that 'governments have to understand that business is not just another pressure group but a resource that will help them set the right rules.'[25] This declaration is prompted by the belief that, on the whole, governments are pandering to activists: '[Governments are] apologising for globalisation and promising to civilise it. Instead, if they had any regard for the plight of the poor, they would be accelerating it, celebrating it, exulting in it – and if all that were too much for the public they would at least be trying to explain it.'[26]

The 'right rules' proposed by groups like the ICC take the form of policies to promote corporate globalization. These policies involve lowering corporate taxes, accommodating international flows of speculative capital, reducing public expenditures, privatizing public services, deregulating business, and securing monopoly private property rights under law.[27] When discussing corporate globalization and the developing world, E. Benjamin Skinner, research associate for U.S. foreign policy at the Council on Foreign Relations, highlights these additional policies:

- Making access to loans cheaper and easier
- Making capital markets more flexible
- Encouraging greater capital flows to the international lower middle classes
- Keeping interest rates low

- Expanding debt and equity markets
- Increasing access to credit through mini- (rather than micro-) lending.[28]

The policies that promote corporate globalization are put in place to allow for increased economic growth. Advocates encourage 'large-scale growth' and 'faster growth' because accelerated growth is seen as the means whereby people can be pulled up into 'gainful employment and dignified sustenance.'[29]

Restrictions on these policies are considered barriers to corporate globalization. For example, any sort of regulation of labour and environmental standards would be 'neoprotectionist' and 'thwart the integration of developing countries into the world economy and discourage trade between poor countries and rich ones.' In addition, trade sanctions imposed on any country 'threaten globalization by disrupting market access and tempting protectionists.'[30]

One of the most prevalent arguments in favour of corporate globalization involves the alleviation of poverty. Dollar and Kraay argue that the current wave of globalization, which started around 1980, has reduced poverty. *The Economist* labels third-world poverty as 'the most pressing moral, political and economic issue of our time.' In answer to this pressing issue, the World Bank declares that 'globalization has helped reduce poverty in a large number of developing countries.'[31] But this reduction of poverty can be obstructed: 'Economic opportunities in the third world would be far greater, and poverty therefore vastly reduced, right now except for barriers to trade – that is, restrictions on economic freedom – erected by rich- and poor-country governments alike.'[32] For advocates of corporate globalization, the benefits of decreased poverty include increased consumption. Skinner maintains that beneficiaries of corporate globalization could be made into consumers as well as producers. In addition, much of the world could become 'more well-rounded – and more affluent – capitalists.'[33]

Opposition to corporate globalization is seen as a 'tragedy in the making,' with protestors depicted as 'rag tag' know-nothing bullies who range from neo-Nazi skinheads through anarchists and non-aligned malcontents to communists.[34] But opposition to corporate globalization is appearing in unexpected quarters. Professor Robert Wade, of the London School of Economics, maintains that the statistics relied on by the pro-globalizers, led by the World Bank, are suspect, and that, on the balance of the evidence, the situation over the last twenty years has been

getting worse under globalization and inequality is increasing.[35] George
Soros, a prominent financier who made millions speculating against the
British pound, laments that 'People increasingly rely on money as the
criterion of value [and] ... what used to be a medium of exchange has
usurped the place of fundamental values.'[36]

Joseph Stiglitz, former chief economist of the World Bank, former
chairman of the Council of Economic Advisors, and winner of the 2001
Nobel Prize for economics, argues that globalization has 'condemned
people to death.' In an extended interview, Stiglitz explained that the
World Bank's careful in-country investigations to create assistance strate-
gies for poor countries consist of a close inspection of those countries'
five-star hotels, concluding in a meeting with some begging, busted
finance minister who signs a restructuring agreement.[37] Each minister is
then handed the same four-step program. The first step is privatization –
which Stiglitz said could more accurately be called 'briberization' – in
which national leaders receive 10 per cent commissions paid to Swiss
bank accounts for every state industry they privatize. The second step is
capital market liberalization, to allow investment capital to flow in and
out. Unfortunately, in what Stiglitz referred to as 'the hot money cycle,'
the money simply flows out and out. When the nation's reserves are
drained, the International Monetary Fund steps in to demand that the
nation raise interest rates to 30 per cent, 50 per cent and 80 per cent,
which predictably, according to Stiglitz, results in demolished property
values, savaged industrial production, and drained national treasuries.
The third step is market-based pricing, which really means raising prices
on food, water, and cooking gas. This third step leads to what Stiglitz calls
'the IMF riot,' which causes new, panicked flights of capital and government bankruptcies, resulting in foreign corporations picking off remaining assets at fire-sale prices. The fourth step is the IMF/World Bank
'poverty reduction strategy': free trade, which Stiglitz compares to the
Opium War. But instead of a military blockade to break open markets,
the World Bank can order a financial blockade. Stiglitz recounted a
meeting, early in his World Bank tenure, with Ethiopia's first democratically elected president. The World Bank and the IMF had ordered
Ethiopia to divert aid money to their account at the U.S. Treasury, which
paid a 4 per cent return, while the nation borrowed U.S. dollars at 12 per
cent to feed its population. The new president begged Stiglitz to let him
use the aid money to rebuild the country, but this was not allowed. What
ultimately drove Stiglitz to put his job on the line, and get fired by the
World Bank, was the failure of the banks and the U.S. Treasury to

change course when confronted with the crises caused by their four-step program. Instead, each time their so-called free market solutions failed, more free market policies were demanded.[38]

Many of those who oppose corporate globalization associate it with the increasing dominance of transnational corporations around the world. Seemingly inescapable, corporate globalization has penetrated most aspects of people's lives, from government policy and school curriculum to public washrooms and rural countrysides. It is a global hegemonic force supported by an ideology of inevitability that precludes discussion of any alternative way of life.

Corporate globalization is based on the money code of value. Living by the money code of value means that money, not life, regulates thought and action. Decisions, whether conscious or unconscious, are based on this overriding value program. It guides choices at every step, creating a matrix of value-laden actions that have profound consequences around the world. A product of such decision-making, corporate globalization is thus not inevitable or natural or God-given. It is the outcome of decisions made in corporate boardrooms, political caucuses, municipal offices, university senates, and hospital meeting rooms. Although deeply entrenched, it is neither irrefutable nor irreversible (nevertheless, its effects on the planet may result in irreversible damage).

Almost by definition, corporate globalization seeks to maximize revenues to corporate stockholders and high-level corporate managers, thereby instantiating the money code of value. In order to accomplish this enrichment, transnational corporations roam the world looking for opportunities for the largest output with the smallest input. Output means profits. Input means costs, including paying fair wages, abiding by environmental regulations, and adhering to health and safety laws. As business competition becomes more global, the ways that different countries account for such costs creates the so-called 'uneven playing field.' Former World Bank senior economist, Herman E. Daly, explains how this difficulty is overcome under corporate globalization: 'The market left to itself will resolve the difficulty by standards-lowering competition– the way of counting costs that results in the cheapest product ... Capital will move to the country that does the least complete job of internalizing environmental and social costs. Consequently, globalization results in a larger share of world product being produced under regimes that externalize costs to the greatest degree.'[39] It is this combination of ever higher profits with ever lower costs that creates the incubus that is corporate globalization. Under its agenda, environmental damage, child labour abuses, massive unemployment, or hazardous workplaces are externalities that must not affect the constant search for the lowest inputs possible.

Generally speaking, corporate globalization involves larger markets – moving from local, regional, national, or international markets to global ones. But something is lost in this transition. The global market bears no resemblance to 'the real free market'[40] that is found in town squares and village streets around the world, but appropriates the same name to domesticate its rapacious activities.

Corporate globalization also involves capital mobility, which changes the emphasis of trade from production commodities to financial ones. Encouraged by fluctuating currency values, capital mobility has resulted in currency trading surpassing the trade in goods and services by more than twenty to one, with foreign currency transactions estimated at $1.3 trillion (U.S.) daily.[41] Such increased capital mobility has made economic well-being ephemeral and transient, with boom-and-bust cycles alternating among different regions and countries.

Corporate globalization also involves greater specialization, encouraged by policies of comparative advantage, which governs trade between nations.[42] While still promoted by global institutions like the International Monetary Fund, in reality comparative advantage is being replaced by 'absolute advantage,' by which global capitalists rather than nations compete with each other for both labourers and natural resources, as well as markets, in all countries.[43]

Although romanticized in the corporate-owned media, corporate globalization has negative consequences for the majority of people in the world. Promoted as a global solution to world problems, it actually leaves life-threatening instability and rising inequality in its wake. In fact, corporate globalization has no place for those who cannot afford to take up the role of the consumer who contributes to corporate profits. Susan George argues that we are in 'the age of exclusion,' when those who cannot afford to join the consumer culture have no right to exist.[44] In this exclusionary dystopia of winners and losers, we are encouraged to emulate the winners – the wealthy – and blame the victims of corporate globalization: the poor. By blaming the victims' situation on their failure to compete successfully in the global market, responsibility for their condition can be avoided. With corporate globalization, responsibility is easy to evade. According to Wendell Berry, the buck never stops when it comes to transnational corporations: 'The buck is processed up the hierarchy until finally it is passed to "the shareholders," who are too widely dispersed, too poorly informed, and too unconcerned to be responsible for anything.'[45]

Among the losers in the casino capitalism that is corporate globalization, according to a United Nations human development report, are 'the 1.3 billion people living on a dollar a day or less, the 160 million malnourished children, the one-fifth of the world's population not expected to live beyond 40, and the 100 million people in the West who are living below the poverty line.'[46]

Such impoverishment is not accidental, nor should it be a surprise. It is the predictable outcome of the money code of value, which selects for money over life – the more money the better, regardless of what happens to life. Life, and indeed the very people mentioned in the United Nations report, are externalities to a system that chooses money over life, promoting a worldview that sees money values as the only values worth pursuing. The grotesque consequences of the money code of value are exemplified in the knowledge that the poor and the marginalized are of no use or interest to those who promote corporate globalization because they are not sites of profit extraction (i.e., consumers). However, as non-voluntary consumers of the increasingly corporatized prison-industrial complex, each one represents a $50,000 to $100,000 annual public payout – the reason why transnational corporations are investing in this growth industry.[47]

All in all, corporate globalization involves globalization organized by the elites, for the elites. As a manifestation of the money code of value, it has wide-ranging but predictable impacts on communities around the world, including rural communities.

Globalization from Below

In response to the impacts of corporate globalization, many forms of resistance have bloomed. Much of this resistance is loosely based on life values that promote an alternative vision for the world. Labelled 'globalization from below,' it aims 'to restore to communities the power to nurture their environments; to enhance the access of ordinary people to the resources they need; to democratize local, national, and transnational political institutions; and to impose pacification on conflicting power centers.'[48]

The term *globalization from below* was first used in 1993 by Richard Falk, professor of international law at Princeton University. Falk sees globalization from below consisting of 'an array of transnational social forces

animated by environmental concerns, human rights, hostility to patriar-
chy, and a vision of human community based on the unity of diverse
cultures seeking an end to poverty, oppression, humiliation, and collective violence.'[49]

In their book, *Global Village or Global Pillage: Economic Reconstruction
from the Bottom Up,* Brecher and Costello compare the power of corporate
globalization to Gulliver as seen by the Lilliputians. Only by working
together could the Lilliputians immobilize Gulliver and prevent his
marauding ways. They argue that globalization from below works in the
same way: 'Only by combining their efforts can those resisting the effects
of globalization in Chicago and Warsaw, Chiapas and Bangalore begin to
bring the New World Economy under control.'[50]

A sample of the groups that make up globalization from below includes workers, women, peasants, indigenous people, and environmentalists, all with diverse, overlapping (although not always complementary)
goals of economic and gender equality, environmental sustainability,
cultural autonomy for diverse peoples, respect for basic human rights,
and democracy.[51] These goals reflect an adherence to the life code of
value because they preserve or extend life's vital range rather than
maintaining and enhancing corporate profits for stockholders. Adherence to the life code of value, whether conscious or unconscious, results
in decisions that are very different from those that follow from the
money code of value. Globalization from below seeks to challenge and
resist the hegemony of corporate globalization, creating alternative ways
of life built on inclusion, interaction, and democratic decision-making.
While there is no doubt that fundamentalist, reactionary versions of
globalization from below exist, the majority involve democratically oriented movements based around life values.

Although diverse and unorganized, globalization from below has common threads that link the various forms of resistance to corporate
globalization. Rather than fusing people into a single identity (such as
global consumer), globalization from below encourages diverse identities while catalysing those common interests that revolve around life
values, such as the environment, equality, and peace. With deep roots in
local struggles, the resistance that characterizes globalization from below is a fairly new phenomenon: 'It is only relatively recently, perhaps
only in the last five or ten years, that activists around the world have
begun to put their local struggles – against environmental damage,
social decay, the destruction of local economies and cultures, the exploi-

tation of labour and so forth – into a global context. Only in the 1990s has resistance, like capital itself, begun to become truly globalised.'[52]

Examples of globalization from below are growing, in both rural and urban areas. An early example of globalization from below involved the coalitions and networks that formed in Mexico, Canada, and the United States to oppose NAFTA. Other examples include the successful campaigning against the Multilateral Agreement on Investment in the mid-1990s, global opposition to the Narmada dam project in India that will dislocate thousands of rural people, global boycotts of Shell Oil for its destruction of the land of the Ogoni people in Nigeria, and the landmark demonstrations against the World Bank and International Monetary Fund in Seattle, Washington, and Quebec City at the turn of the century.

The importance of globalization from below lies in its ability to construct and legitimize alternatives to corporate globalization. Judith Marshall sees the power of alternatives that globalization from below can offer when she discusses trade union connections in the globalized economy:

> In this new era, then, workers will either be haplessly played off against each other as rights and standards fall to the lowest common denominator, or find ways to work in concert to level rights and standards upwards. This means strengthened institutional capacity, both in the North and the South, to globalize from below, working together to invent alternatives that create jobs and communities, affirm equity and diversity, and promote sustainable development.[53]

These alternatives offer a vision that is qualitatively different from the urbanized, consumerist homogeneity offered by corporate globalization. Based on life values, that vision would place individual and community well-being, and the natural environment we depend on, above corporate profit.

Part of that vision could be the formation of a *global civil society*, a term first used by Stephen Gill in 1991. In an article entitled 'Reflections on Global Order and Sociohistorical Time,' Gill discusses

> the new potential for counterhegemonic and progressive forces to begin to make transnational links, and thereby to insert themselves in a more differentiated, multilateral world order. This would be a way to advance the

process of the democratization of an emerging global civil society and system of international political authority, currently monopolized by the forces of transnational capital, the governments of the major states, and supervised by the Bretton Woods institutions and the military alliances of the West. This might then provide the political space and social possibility to begin to mobilize for the solution to deep-seated global problems of social inequality, intolerance, environmental depredation, and the militarization of the planet.[54]

Formed partly as a response to the vacuum in leadership created when governments signed away many of the democratic rights of their citizens and their own national businesses, global civil society is a 'space where things happen. It is not an actor itself. It is the place where social movement organizations, international research and advocacy networks, global policy bodies as well as a wide variety of non-governmental (NGO) and international non-governmental organizations (INGO) interact with states, the United Nations and other intergovernmental bodies and the private sector itself. It is a political space which has grown in response to and in resistance to the globalizing forces of the day.'[55]

The essence of global civil society is networking, which consists of at least the following types of activities: research on skills, needs, interests of network members; face-to-face meetings; national, regional, continental, or international events; exchange of letters; telephone conversations; fax exchanges; newsletter or bulletin services; publications and exchange of materials; and electronic mail systems using computers.[56] Networking is essential not only to promote awareness about corporate globalization, but also to build bridges and consensus between diverse and widely dispersed organizations in rural communities, as well as in urban areas.

Global civil society is based on the concept of civil society – a contested term in current understanding. Seen by some as the solution to our current problems, the concept of *civil society* is often romanticized as the new political arena. But the very flabbiness of a term like civil society prompted critics like Antonio Gramsci to look at it more closely. For Gramsci, *civil society* – 'the ensemble of organisms commonly called "private"' – was part of the superstructure, along with *political society* (i.e., the State).[57] Far from romantic, it was primarily, but not exclusively, a site of hegemony. Following Gramsci's understanding, civil society in Canada would encompass not only the Council of Canadians, but also the Canadian Council of Chief Executives (formerly the Business Council on

National Issues), while global civil society would encompass not only Greenpeace, but also the World Trade Organization. How can we differentiate between these extremes and find a meaningful role for global civil society to play in creating alternatives to corporate globalization?

Peter Mayo helps us answer this question when he contends that civil society is regarded as an area that, for the most part, consolidates, through its dominant institutions, the existing hegemonic arrangements, but which also contains sites or pockets, often within the dominant institutions themselves, wherein these arrangements are constantly renegotiated and contested.[58]

The existing hegemonic arrangements in most countries today involve corporate globalization, driven by the money code of value. Those who work out of the life code of value are challenging these arrangements through sites or pockets within civil society, and, increasingly, within global civil society. But it is not enough to simply challenge the existing hegemonic arrangements – counter-hegemony can also be driven by the money code of value. The challenge must come through the life code of value in order to be part of the search for sustainability. In this way, both the Council of Canadians and Greenpeace, by working from the life code of value, could play a meaningful role in building alternatives to corporate globalization, while the Canadian Council of Chief Executives and the World Trade Organization could not, unless spaces opened up within these organizations where the life code of value could operate.

This chapter has examined the history of globalization and investigated the two major manifestations of globalization that directly affect sustainability: corporate globalization and globalization from below. Although it is the dominant form of globalization today, corporate globalization is being challenged by globalization from below, in the form of transnational networks and strategic alliances among grassroots groups and their allies. If they are founded on the life code of value and 'operationalized' through global civil society, the emergence of these networks and alliances signals a new opportunity to counter the destructive impacts of corporate globalization. Before exploring this opportunity, we need to examine these impacts, which are felt around the world, but nowhere more acutely than at the local level – especially in rural communities.

2 Rural Reckoning: The Impacts of Corporate Globalization on Rural Communities

The globalizers of the economy will be treated with more severity than ...
Sodom and Gomorrah, which already is a rather strong threat to those who
in their arrogance think that well-being is only for a few and exclude the rest
forever.[1]

Corporate globalization is a worldwide phenomenon that has rapidly
come to affect the lives of many people – rich and poor, women and
men, urban and rural. Its impact is felt not only at the level of the nation
state, but in communities and households as well. While some hail its
arrival, others fear its totalitarian rule. Working from an interdisciplinary range of research studies that span a twenty-year period, this chapter will outline the economic, political, social, environmental, gendered,
and cultural effects of corporate globalization on rural communities.
The evidence clearly indicates that corporate globalization has had
devastating consequences for rural communities both in Canada and
around the world.

The impact of corporate globalization has been overwhelmingly negative for a growing number of people. While economic growth in countries such as Indonesia, Taiwan, and Thailand was championed as the
miracle of the Asian Tigers, the subsequent Asian Meltdown put an end
to such naive optimism. In Canada, fishing villages, farm communities,
northern settlements, and mining towns are reeling from resource depletion, corporate consolidation, government cutbacks, and industry shutdowns. The reality, for many in 'the Majority World,' is grim, with little
relief in sight. All in all, the consequences of corporate globalization are
becoming a global disaster.

Driven by money values that tolerate no boundaries, corporate global-ization has penetrated every region on the globe, with similar results: 'The impact of the global economy is essentially the same wherever you are in the world. It merely manifests itself in different ways, according to the local context. So the analysis of what is happening in remote villages in India and to cities in Britain or Japan is virtually identical.'[2]

Although corporate globalization does not discriminate between rural and urban areas, its impact on rural communities plays out in very special ways. Sparsely populated and spatially isolated, rural commu-nities lack the range and depth of resources available to their urban counterparts to deal with these impacts. In addition, they are often excluded from consideration by the urban bias written into government programs and policies.

In Canada, these rural vulnerabilities have a long history, beginning with European colonization and the development of a staples economy. Over the intervening centuries, what J.M.S. Careless calls the metropolis or dominant large city could effectively dominate wide economic hinter-lands, whether adjacent or remote, on a number of levels: 'Moreover, the policy decisions, the stores of knowledge, and the techniques that were concentrated in such a commanding city were transmitted outward to the hinterland, working to organize it not in economic terms alone, but in political and social systems, cultural institutions, and built envi-ronments as well.'[3]

While history makes it clear that the metropolis and the hinterland benefited from each other, the relationships between them were not equitable: 'Hinterland societies assuredly might come to perceive their lot as one of subservience and exploitation, as pawns of high-powered city interests, and they recurrently expressed this view in frontier and regional protest movements.' Exploitation of hinterland resources, Care-less argued, could lead to their depletion or exhaustion as the 'ravaging march of progress' resulted in despoiled farmlands, clear-cut forests, or abandoned mines and settlements. In this way, 'popular images of the ruthless big city and the victimized countryside reflected the plain per-ceptions of inequity.'[4]

In Canada before 1914, Careless saw the relationships between metropolis and hinterland as essentially 'relations between a dominant urban power centre and its supplying, serviced territory.' During the twentieth century, modern industrialism and growing economic nation-alism resulted in what Harold Innis described as 'the increasing disparity between standards of living of urban and rural populations.'[5] Today, the escalating demands of flexible accumulation characteristic of corporate globalization require every hinterland and metropolis to compete with every other hinterland and metropolis around the world. This hyper-competitive environment catches many countries, and many rural communities, in what could be called a modern version of the classic 'staple trap,' described so well by Daniel Drache in his edited volume of Harold Innis's work:

> The vast wealth generated from the staple trades went hand in hand with a crippling pattern of commercial dependency that shaped the fundamental condition of Canadian development. The wealth from resources, the revenues from markets, and the benefits from production flowed largely to others. This was because Canada's economic trajectory was subject to the decisions and strategies of states or groups within the dominant industrial countries. Development governed by such external constraints resulted in sudden overspecialization in one or two sectors of the economy while other sectors faced limited growth prospects.[6]

While it is clear that many of the problems facing rural areas are global in their origins, the impacts of what has come to be known as corporate globalization on rural communities in Canada and elsewhere are profoundly local in nature. The responses to these impacts, in turn, are complex and vastly differentiated, given the heterogeneity of rural communities themselves. While some passively accept their lot and struggle to adapt to the demands of the global market, others resist and try to shape external forces to local requirements. For example, when studying local responses to global change, Norcliffe found that despite commonalities in the pattern of restructuring within three prominent pulp and paper mills, there were important differences related to the local circumstances in each mill. Overall, he concluded, the tension between global capital and transnational corporations operating on a largely deregulated playing field, on the one hand, and local players defending their own patch of turf, on the other, results in each place moulding larger socio-economic processes into place-specific outcomes and provides the richness in much of the recent research in the social sciences.[7]

Research conducted in rural communities over a twenty-year period reveals a range of impacts associated with corporate globalization. These impacts can be divided into economic, political, social, environmental, gendered, and cultural impacts that overlap in a web of interrelatedness. This interrelatedness is illustrated by Maureen Reed's description of transition in forestry communities: 'Since the mid-1970s, the inevitable decline of timber availability associated with the fall-down effect, changes in international market conditions, increased mechanization in both harvesting and processing sectors, corporate restructuring, flexible forms of production, increasing public awareness of and demands for environmental protection and wilderness areas, and changes in relations with First Nations have generated challenges to the sustainability of the communities that have developed around forestry on Canada's West Coast.'[8] For the purposes of this analysis, however, separation of these impacts will help to better understand how corporate globalization affects rural communities.

Economic Impacts

In rural communities, the economic impacts of corporate globalization are eroding the very foundations of the rural way of life. As the money values of corporate globalization are increasingly felt in rural communities, the life values of co-operation, loyalty, sharing, mutual obligation, trust, and solidarity are being downgraded or pushed aside.

Traditionally resource-based, rural communities have long produced primary products and provided local employment. With the rise of corporate globalization in the 1980s, rural areas dependent on agriculture, mining, and natural resource industries began to experience severe economic stress. And as the 1980s turned into the 1990s and the internationalization of the world economy increasingly occurred through finance, 'capital markets, rather than commodity markets, appear to be the ultimate determinants of rural welfare and rural social, as well as economic, structures.'[9]

To understand the increasing dominance of capital markets under corporate globalization, we need to understand the imperatives of capital itself. Harvey describes capitalism as 'always about growth, no matter what the ecological, social or geopolitical consequences (indeed, we define 'crisis' as low growth).' He sees this drive for growth reflected in the transformation of urban governance from 'managerialism to entrepreneurialism,' and expressed in growth-machine politics. For Harvey, urban entrepreneurialism means 'that pattern of behavior within urban governance that mixes together state powers (local, metropolitan, regional, national or supranational) and a wide array of organizational forms in civil society (chambers of commerce, unions, churches, educational and research institutions, community groups, NGOs, and the like) and private interests (corporate and individual) to form coalitions to promote or manage urban/regional development of some sort or other.'[10] We can extend Harvey's understanding of the imperatives of capital to posit a corresponding rural entrepreneurialism that operates as the new form of governance in rural communities. For just as 'urban governance has moved more rather than less into line with the naked requirements of capital accumulation,' rural governance has followed suit, assuming 'an entrepreneurial stance [that] contrasts with the managerial practices of earlier decades which primarily focussed on the local provision of services, facilities and benefits' to rural populations.[11]

Clare Mitchell's research into rural communities reinforces this extension of Harvey's understanding of the imperatives of capital. She reminds us that the driving force behind capitalism is the quest for surplus value or profit, adding that once initiated by an entrepreneur, the process of capital accumulation is almost impossible to stop. It follows, therefore, that entrepreneurs, driven to accumulate capital, continuously seek out investment opportunities, and that 'restricting one's investment in the face of escalating profits ... is counter-intuitive to the entrepreneurial mindset.'[12]

Mitchell's insights into the imperatives of capital in rural community development reflect the earlier work of Trevor J. Barnes and Roger Hayter in their study of the forestry community of Chemainus, British Columbia. Using the work of David Harvey and Harold Innis to frame their understanding of the process of capital accumulation, they found that 'In many ways the economic geographical history of forest products in British Columbia is a history of creative destruction. The forestry resource towns that form the backbone of the province's economy literally come and go – are created and annihilated – in the cyclonic ferocity of the accumulation process. In this sense such communities are the fulcrum connecting wider economic changes with those on the ground.'[13] Overall, the imperatives of capital underlying the economic impacts of corporate globalization affect rural communities through an interconnecting matrix of agro-industrialization, poverty and debt creation, restructuring, deregulation, privatization, changes in employment/unemployment patterns and commodification/consumption.

Agro-industrialization

While farming has always been a difficult occupation, it has become almost impossible in the age of globalization for small and medium-sized farms to survive. According to David Suzuki, it's been a long battle by corporations to turn agriculture into agribusiness. Darrin Qualman agrees, adding that the corporate takeover of agriculture is one of the last battles in a long war over who will own the economy – local families or distant investors. In the words of Professor Emeritus of Agricultural Economics, John Ikerd, 'agriculture as we have known it, with family farms and viable rural communities, is being rapidly transformed into an industrial agriculture, with factory farms and dying rural communities.'[14]

The industrialization of agriculture involves massive chemical and biological inputs, monoculturing, habitat destruction, factory farming, and centralized corporate ownership. This industrialization has resulted in severe declines in the number of farms and in the number of people employed in agriculture, with devastating effects for many rural communities. Increasingly, small and medium-sized farms are being replaced by large, agro-industrial farms that are supported by off-farm capital and employing hired labour. Marked by vertically and horizontally integrated production, processing, and distribution of generic inputs for mass marketable foodstuffs, these large, industrial farms are replacing classic family farming.[15]

In Canada, rural communities reflect the new tensions in agriculture, with farmers wanting to feed the world while making a fair income, and others seeing agriculture as a capital-intensive, high-technology, international industry. Such tensions lead one Canadian farmer to voice what many are feeling: if farm land is 'taken over by the corporate farms, there's no doubt that there would be no communities left to speak of.' This scenario becomes more pressing when we realize that in North Dakota, vast tracts of corporate farmland lie 'undisturbed' by farms or communities, while in rural Manitoba, county roads have been ploughed up to create 10,000-acre fields, with no houses in sight.[16]

Agro-industrialization affects rural communities in other ways as well. For example, international trade agreements promote production for export instead of local consumption. Production for export has already created problems in Latin America, where the process of corporate globalization has resulted in an export strategy of fresh fruits and vegetables that promotes local poverty and hunger. In Canada, the National Farmers Union reminds us that increased exports also mean increased imports. With commodity prices set in Calcutta rather than Calgary, Canadian farmers are experiencing a severe income crisis, remaining price-takers rather than price-setters in the international market. This crisis is compounded by a low-cost food policy that externalizes the environmental, health, and social costs of producing food while subsidizing large, corporate players.[17] In addition, the growth of corporate food firms and international finance capital creates a globalized food system that can pit countries against each other in a race to lower standards and eliminate regulations, such as those that even out the comparative costs of rural living.

Either nations choose to protect rural people and are bypassed by transnational investors, or they eliminate the so-called barriers to trade and remove such protections, leaving rural people to face the whims of corporate globalization alone. Summing up 50 years of research in the area of agro-industrialization, Lobao concludes that 'the bulk of evidence indicates that public concern about the detrimental community impacts of industrialized farming is warranted.'[18]

Poverty and Debt Creation

Poverty and debt often go hand in hand, especially in rural communities. When describing how poverty is perpetuated in rural communities by those who benefit from the status quo, Duncan uses Townsend's definition of poverty: the lack of the resources necessary to permit participation in the activities, customs, and diets commonly approved by society.[19]

One of the ways of widening the gap between rich and poor and contributing to poverty is debt creation. Whether it is individual or governmental indebtedness, third-world or first-world indebtedness, all serve to keep money flowing to the wealthiest sectors of the population. While American and Canadian household debt has risen to a new record level of over 90 per cent of after-tax income, government debt has also risen in almost every country in the world. In developed countries, the national debt was deliberately created to 'cap social spending,' allowing the private sector to move into formerly public-sector areas like health care. In developing countries, indebtedness was encouraged as part of 'development.' As country after country found themselves unable to repay their debts, structural adjustment programs (SAPs) were imposed by the World Bank and the International Monetary Fund, which downgraded national priorities such as welfare enhancement while opening the door to foreign investment and export production. These SAPs also forced a change in production, from subsistence farming to export-oriented farming so that national governments could pay interest on their foreign debt. This change in production left many rural families in developing countries unable to feed themselves.[20] In Canada, SAPs were also imposed, but under such euphemisms as 'belt tightening,' 'deficit reduction,' and 'rationalization.' The results were seen in increased levels of bankruptcies, unemployment, and homelessness.

High prices and cheap credit in the 1970s encouraged agricultural indebtedness: 'the good farmer was the highly leveraged farmer.' But a worldwide recession and the farm crisis of the 1980s resulted in a higher value for the dollar, which in turn meant loans were more expensive to pay off and commodity prices on the world market were less competitive for rural producers. Faced with rising debt costs and lower incomes, many either had to expand their operations and go deeper into debt, or sell out. For many farmers, years of borrowing to survive resulted in 'entrenched indebtedness ... and the accompanying rural poverty and inability either to escape from indebtedness or to sell up without walking off the farm penniless.' In this way, the farm crisis of the 1980s not only resulted in economic hardship for many rural families, but also forced many of those same rural families to 'continue to labor under the bonds of economic hardship into the 1990s.'[21]

Agriculture is not the only sector of the rural economy that faces entrenched poverty. Freudenburg's study of the nine most northeastern states of the United States found the highest levels of poverty not in counties dependent on America's best-known declining industry, namely agriculture, nor in those that were dependent on the notoriously low-wage industry of tourism, but in those dependent on two types of extraction that are normally seen as contributing more positively to economic strength, namely forestry and mining. And in his research, Ciccantell found that the restructuring of Canadian mining communities brought on by corporate globalization resulted in local governmental debt and increased poverty.[22]

Restructuring

Restructuring is a blanket term often used to describe changes in the economy, such as downsizing, stagnant wages, and increased part-time jobs. Foley warns that restructuring should be understood as a myth that masks the actual processes of capital reorganization. He adds that any economic restructuring which is directed by the capitalist state will be, ultimately and primarily, in the interests of capital and against the general interest. His view of the consequences of economic restructuring is borne out by McMichael, who argues that when states restructure, they may improve their financial standing and their export sectors, but the majority of citizens and poorer classes find their protections shorn away in the rush to participate in the world market.[23]

Restructuring has had a devastating impact on the economies of rural areas, especially those communities that depend on manufacturing. Demanded in the name of economic efficiency, restructuring creates cascading repercussions. For example, in the western Australian wheatbelt, rural restructuring has resulted in significant changes in the employment structure, with the primary sector of the workforce declining by 30 per cent. This decline contributed to the process of depopulation, which has resulted in many rural communities struggling to survive. In addition, rural restructuring has resulted in the withdrawal of services and the contraction of local economies.[24]

The fiscal impacts of restructuring in the United States are emphasized by Flora and Flora, who contend that the economic restructuring facing rural America has led to decreasing incomes and a decreasing tax base in many areas. Restructuring is impoverishing small ranchers and farmers, forcing them to sell out, depopulating large chunks of rural America and changing the way Americans get their food. A study of displaced workers in the United States revealed that rural workers were more likely to be displaced and experienced higher economic costs following displacement than urban workers. This study reflects the findings of other studies of rural counties in the United States, where economic restructuring in the 1980s resulted in employment problems. For example, Duncan and Lamborghini found that the coal counties of Appalachia lost 2,000 mining jobs, while northern New England counties lost 1,000 manufacturing jobs.[25]

In Canada, restructuring has also taken its toll on rural communities. The logical outcome of the processes of restructuring, according to Glen Norcliffe, is the bifurcation of the Canadian labour market, understood as 'a *decline* in middle-income blue-collar jobs, coupled with the *growth* of, on the one hand, skilled scientific, managerial, and professional jobs and, on the other hand, low-paid service-sector jobs.' The so-called 'good jobs' are located mainly in metropolitan areas, while the growing proportion of 'bad jobs,' heavily concentrated in retail and personal services, are well represented in the periphery.[26]

Corporate concentration, a hallmark of restructuring, has not only affected prairie farm communities, but also dramatically shaped the destinies of northern logging towns, with consolidation in the logging, sawmill, and pulp and paper sectors forcing closures. Restructuring in coal-mining communities in western Canada due to corporate globalization brought on hard times for the people who lived there. As a result of restructuring, these communities experienced a decline of one-third in average incomes, lower local spending of wages, stalled residential development and construction, and empty shopping malls.[27]

All in all, one recent study concluded, any private-sector or public-sector restructuring that takes place as a result of globalization impacts differently and more severely on rural communities than on their urban and metropolitan counterparts. Such restructuring engenders the kind of endless, grinding poverty that prompted one rancher to comment: 'If you pass on your ranch to your son ... then it's child abuse.'[28]

Deregulation

To facilitate capital accumulation in a global market, capital requires freedom from regulation and so-called state interference in the market. In essence, the process of deregulation involves the removal or reduction of constraints upon the operation of the free market, particularly affecting the free entry of competitors into areas previously controlled by monopolies or dominant firms and agencies. This process, however, 'bids fair to widen the gap between basically profitable and unprofitable sectors and places, and between rich and poor.'[29]

One unspoken aspect of the drive for deregulation is re-regulation, but by the rules drawn up by the representatives of transnational corporations, not by democratically elected governments. Accompanying the dismantling of decades of regulations designed to protect the public from the excesses of capital is a systematic enforcement of regulations that favour transnational business activities, of which the North American Free Trade Agreement (NAFTA) is but one example.

In this vein, the new rules proposed by the Uruguay Round that challenge agricultural protection and farm subsidies will result in a streamlining of agriculture that can only accelerate farm concentration and de-ruralization trends, resulting in 'making the rural even more intensely residual,' but on a global scale.[30]

New Zealand provides a classic study of deregulation.[31] In that country, deregulation included two kinds of reforms: macroeconomic reforms, such as the floating of the exchange rate and removal of import licences; and sectoral reforms, including deregulation of the agricultural sector. This deregulation dismantled the structure of subsidies, tax and other fiscal incentives, and the price controls that had been built up to protect farmers. Although initially welcomed by farmers, agricultural deregulation was shortly followed by falling world commodity prices, worsening terms of trade, and rising interest rates and inflation, all of which meant that farmers were faced with dramatically reduced incomes and land values on one hand, and rising debts on the other. At the community level, deregulation had a number of impacts in New Zealand. It resulted in the acceleration of the centralization of services in larger centres, which directly affects rural community members' access to those services. In addition, one study found that deregulation altered the relationship between businesses and the farming community: traditionally based on loyalty, that relationship is now based on competitiveness, which has long-term implications for the survival of rural communities.

Privatization

Another economic impact of corporate globalization involves the privatization of the public sector in order to create new markets for private investment and profit. The 'neologism of privatization' in contemporary parlance means organizing private-sector accumulation with public-sector funds. While numerous excuses are put forward to justify privatization, the whole point of privatization is neither economic efficiency nor improved services to the consumer but 'simply to transfer wealth from the public purse – which could redistribute it to even out social inequalities – to private hands.'[32]

Privatization shifts responsibilities from the state to the market. As a democratic institution, the state was obliged to at least consider the welfare of all citizens, regardless of distant location. Not so with the market, which will only invest in areas of assured profit. As a result, privatization has resulted in reduced service in rural areas. Public services in danger of privatization include postal services, public utilities, telecommunications, and public transport, all of which are crucial to the well-being of rural communities. In addition, the remoteness of many rural communities from privatized water, gas, and electrical supplies 'might thereby incur disproportionate increases.' As well, the extension of privatization into education and health services will not only have a 'major distributional impact' on the rural deprived, but will also have detrimental effects on the labour force as public-sector national wage rates are replaced by locally bargained (and traditionally lower) rural wage rates.[33]

An ideology of self-help promotes the privatization agenda. Hailed as 'dependency reduction and innovation stimulus,' privatization ultimately demands that the rural community, not the private corporation, replace the state as provider of particular functions. All in all, privatization will not serve rural areas well, as a whole, and will disadvantage 'the least affluent rural people.'[34]

Changes in Employment/Unemployment Patterns

Yet another economic impact of corporate globalization involves changes in employment and unemployment patterns, such as indentured, child, and slave labour, 'flexible' employment, and increased unemployment. As competition intensifies in the global market, full-time, stable employment dwindles, while new forms of employment, and unemployment, increase.

In general, corporate globalization undermines employment opportunities. As transnational corporations roam the globe looking for the lowest costs, hard-won labour laws in developed countries are bypassed in favour of low-wage, or no-wage, alternatives in developing countries. Unemployment mushrooms while the social safety net is shredded, all in the name of economic efficiency. The resulting loss of jobs represents 'the "hollowing out" of a nation's economic base, and the erosion of social institutions that stabilize the conditions of employment and habitat associated with those jobs.'[35]

Like many other communities around the world, rural communities have suffered from the changes in employment and unemployment patterns brought on by corporate globalization. Fordist traditions of stable, well-paid, full-time, unionized work evaporate as more and more corporations look for labour 'flexibility,' which Leach and Winson refer to as 'a euphemism for cutting their wage bill.' In rural America, for example, McLaughlin, Gardner, and Lichter found that recent economic restructuring, which is characteristic of corporate globalization, has gone 'hand-in-hand with the erosion of employment opportunities.'[36]

Under corporate globalization, Marsden finds conventional categories and formal boundaries of rural labour becoming increasingly redundant. He sees more emphasis on variable time and activity patterns, more casual and freelance work, variable leisure patterns, the erosion of the distinctiveness of domestic and formal labour, and more 'hire and fire' vulnerability. He adds that recent analyses suggest that these new forms of labour activity are characterized by 'higher levels of exploitation and declining levels of social rights.'[37]

More and more, employment falls into two categories: one small category with well-paid, highly skilled work; and a much larger category with unskilled, precarious work. The latter category includes workers who have suffered what Leach and Winson refer to as 'occupational skidding' – a slide to lower paying, often part-time work with limited fringe benefits and a decline of quality of life on the job. Such dualistic labour processes, Marsden contends, may be more pronounced in rural regions, with a small proportion of white-collar workers and 'a large proportion of blue-collar workers' jobs being down-graded and de-skilled in a "secondary" labour sector.'[38]

Yet another change in employment patterns involves the rise of the service industry, which has replaced the manufacturing that moved to low-wage countries. The decline of well-paid, unionized employment has paved the way for low-wage service jobs. These low-wage jobs demand either long or intermittent hours, involve poor working conditions, promote de-skilling, provide few, if any, benefits, and offer little chance of advancement. In many parts of the world, such service jobs are becoming increasingly concentrated in major urban areas and global cities, leaving rural communities behind.

Even those rural areas able to host the service industry experience unexpected impacts. Recent research in the United States has shown that the rural counties facing the greatest socio-economic and family structure problems were the counties that were dependent on the service industry, and, far from solving their economic problems, the service industry may be fuelling additional ones.[39]

One sector of the growing service industry is the tourist industry, which is promoted as a replacement for the manufacturing jobs lost because of corporate globalization. As rural communities find themselves competing with one another for tourist dollars, it is important to recognize the downside of the tourism bonanza. While investments in tourism can generate significant benefits for some people involved in rural tourism, 'such investments have also led to a partial destruction of the rural idyll, to the loss of a community that is happy, healthy and problem-free.'[40]

In addition, the quality of employment in the tourism industry, like the rest of the service industry, is a poor substitute for the jobs lost through corporate globalization. According to Coates, 'Tourism is often touted as a viable alternative, although the lower wages and seasonality of this sector combine with comparatively small markets and intense national and international competition to make tourism an uncertain foundation for regional prosperity.'[41]

Another change in employment patterns involves working off the farm. While off-farm work is not new to the agricultural sector, such work has increased as an adaptive strategy by farm families facing severely reduced incomes. Typical of many countries, increasing numbers of farm households in New Zealand 'reduced their reliance on farm incomes by one or other partner working off the farm.' By 1999, in the United States, almost 90 per cent of household income for American farm populations came from non-farm sources.[42]

The rate of unemployment has also increased due to corporate globalization. In this era of the 'jobless recovery,' the economy thrives while more and more people face destitution. McMurtry explains the role of unemployment under corporate globalization: Unemployment and loss of livelihood to people is a further benefit to transnational operations and businesses in general because it lowers the price of labour, and, therefore, the revenues that private employers are required to pay out to workers.[43]

In Canada, Norcliffe found that a restructured staples economy dominated by foreign ownership has resulted in increased cyclicality of employment in most resource industries, with the partial exception of agriculture. The changes show up in the levels of unemployment as well as in fluctuations in the supply of labour. In single-industry communities, for example, a labour force may migrate in and then disperse, without the unemployment rate ever rising very much. But in more stable communities, the downsizing or complete closure of a mine or sawmill may lead to very high unemployment rates. He concludes that older forms of 'Fordist' labour-market segmentation are being replaced in resource-based regions of the hinterland with a core segment that is *functionally* flexible among different tasks and enjoys considerable job security, and a secondary segment that is *numerically* flexible, depending on levels of economic activity.[44]

According to Leach and Winson, there is strong evidence of a rather substantial and disturbing increase in the proportion of unemployed individuals experiencing long-term unemployment. Such long-term unemployment carries high social and individual costs: for society, it leads to marginalization of a segment of the labour force and higher costs for unemployment insurance and other social programs; for the individual, it leads to erosion of work skills, limited prospects, and undermined morale.[45] In the United States, Swaim found that the rural unemployment rate rose more than the urban rate in the recession at the beginning of the 1980s and has remained higher ever since.[46]

Both lumber and mining communities suffered massive unemployment during the 1980s, from which many never recovered. Berry reports that a large, exploitative absentee economy promotes such practices as 'rape and run' logging; and in Montana, that one logging company levelled entire forests, then quit the state, 'leaving behind hundreds of unemployed mill workers, towns staggered by despair and more than 1,000 square miles of heavily logged land.' In British Columbia, Barnes and Hayter estimate that more than 23,000 people lost their jobs in the forest industry, and, at the bottom of the depression in 1982, over 50 per cent of all loggers, between 25 and 30 per cent of all workers in sawmills, and 60 per cent of shake and shingle workers were unemployed. In farming communities, the level of unemployment can be gauged by the CBC news report in early 2000 that one-third of the farmers in the province of Saskatchewan would be out of business within one year. As communities in the Canadian North struggle to identify opportunities for economic growth and job creation, Coates argues that corporate insistence that Canadian firms match international prices 'has added to labour-management strife, forced the closure of several industrial plants, and otherwise caused economic calamities across the North.'[47]

Commodification/Consumption

Commodification and consumption are essential aspects of corporate globalization, a twin dynamic that can produce the profits that investors restlessly seek. While by no means new concepts, they have gained in significance as the economy has gone global.

Commodification entails turning objects into commodities so they can be exchanged and a profit can be realized. According to Thrift, the process of commodification has reached into every nook and cranny of modern life: in Western societies practically every human activity relies on or has certain commodities associated with it; and in non-Western societies, the process of commodification has increasingly taken hold.[48]

Marsden expands on our understanding of commodification when he explains that it involves the extension of the commodity form to new spheres of activity, brought about by capital's systematic seeking to 'transform use values into exchange values and simultaneously to develop new "needs" and markets.' He contends that successive bouts of re-commodification which transform use values and outdated exchange values are pivotal to the understanding of agrarian change.[49]

In this vein, Mitchell discusses 'the commodification of the country-side ideal,' which involves, first, the idealization of the rural landscape, and, second, the commodification of this myth through mechanisms such as heritage shopping centres. Such commodification has led to problems in rural communities. Newcomers who arrive to live out the countryside ideal can be at odds with long-time residents over issues like pesticide use and manure spreading.[50]

Commodification has also threatened family farms. Blanc argues that because it induces a tendency towards individuation of family members and the severing of work links from affectual ones, commodification weakens one of the main strengths of the family farm: the ability to call on a flexible and cheap workforce from the household. In addition, the context of commodification that is accelerated under corporate globalization increases the value of capital transferred to the successor of the family farm, leaving other children less willing to accept a violation of equity and therefore problematizing the transfer of the family business.[51]

Once commodified, an object needs a consumer to realize a profit for the investor. And while the money values of corporate globalization promote ever-increasing consumption, such a perspective begs the question concerning what happens to the increasing numbers of people around the world who lack the money to enable them to join the consumer culture.

One aspect of the increased scope for consumption is the consumption of rurality itself. This form of consumption affects rural communities in several ways. For example, tourism can involve the consumption of the commodified countryside. Heritage shopping villages become centres of consumption for tourists hungry to purchase a piece of the countryside ideal, which can result in significant tensions between visitors and local residents as tourists flood in to experience that ideal.[52]

Increased consumption also affects rural communities through agricultural production. Ward et al. contend that the role of agricultural production is diminishing in association with a secular redefinition of the social functions of rural space to encompass distinctive consumption roles (such as residence, recreation, leisure, and environmental conservation). Marsden agrees, seeing a decline in the 'productivist system of agriculture' at the same time as the development of a much more diverse set of 'privatized consumption relations.' These privatized consumption relations involve an increase in the personal consumption of goods and services sold by the private sector. Such consumption relations, he warns, are accompanied by the state-supported diminution of the remaining vestiges of collective consumption and welfare.[53]

Jones and Tonts also express concern for rural communities in the face of increased consumption. They argue that the perception of the countryside as a 'space of consumption' to be enjoyed by tourists must be balanced by constructions of the countryside as a 'space of production' – where economic efficiency and ecological sustainability must be maintained – and as a 'space of social action' – where the social values of equity and community can be fostered.[54]

The twin dynamic of commodification and consumption has serious homogenizing impacts on local cultures, including rural cultures. The mass marketing of such commodities as food, music, and clothing is designed to prompt mass consumption responses, which renders local alternatives quaint, at best, but more often simply unfashionable and undesirable. These homogenizing impacts, however, can be dialectically leavened by the effects of local cultures themselves. In his article, 'Commodity Cultures: The Traffic in Things,' Peter Jackson calls for a nuanced response to the cultural complexities of commodification, arguing that the significance that is attached to specific commodities differs markedly from one place to another, according to their contexts of production and consumption. Nigel Thrift agrees, maintaining that new forms of local culture are being produced, along with new meanings of what counts as 'local.'[55] While this more complex engagement with the commodification and consumption dynamic helps us to better understand the economic impacts of corporate globalization on rural communities, it is important to keep in mind that putting corporate commodities to unexpected uses through 'creative consumption' still buys into the growth imperative of the global economy. It is not just any local response that will come to the aid of rural communities, but a response that has the potential to promote sustainability that will make a difference.

By contributing to the growing gap between rich and poor through agro-industrialization, poverty and debt creation, restructuring, deregulation, privatization, changes in employment and unemployment patterns, and commodification/consumption, corporate globalization results in a wide range of economic problems for rural communities.

Political Impacts

The role of the nation state has changed dramatically under corporate globalization, affecting rural communities both directly and indirectly. This changing role involves the erosion of the power of the nation state, which transforms institutions of the state from being protectors of the health and rights of people to protectors of the property and profits of corporations.[56]

The emphasis on corporate globalization has meant that economic policies take precedence over social and environmental policies, resulting in new national priorities such as boosting export production, attracting foreign investment, and rolling back the public sector. In addition, corporate tax avoidance, facilitated by changes in national taxation legislation and lack of regulation at the global level, results in even less money being available for national expenditures such as education and health care.

Corporate globalization has not been matched by political globalization, or a system of governance that can control its powerful forces.[57] While the nation state has traditionally buffered civil society from the excesses of capital, there is no such protection at the global level. Indeed, nation states have fallen over themselves to pave the way for corporate globalization, while undercutting their own ability to respond to transnational corporate demands by signing trade agreements that simply benefit large corporate players. One example of a trade agreement that benefitted a large corporate player involved the rewriting of the forestry law in Mexico to fit the conditions placed on Mexico under the NAFTA treaty. The new forestry bill undermined rural people because it privileged large-scale industrial plantations over native forest management and cut off organized peasants from government aid (extension work, credit, and protected markets). In short, the new law gave incentives exclusively to market-friendly forest development.[58]

As neoliberal economics demand a reduction of state benefits and protections, many governments are adopting less regulatory economic policies. This deregulation results in a loss of sovereignty, because the ability of many governments to deal with national issues through regulatory policy frameworks is restricted. Government policy that does get introduced within this new political climate has serious implications for rural communities because 'rural areas provide less healthy arenas for competition than their urban counterparts.'[59] Reflecting the imperatives of corporate globalization, these policies include public-sector cutbacks, tariff reductions, changes in tax structures, curtailments of rural services, a culture of enterprise, and an ideology of self-reliance.

In New Zealand, for example, the government embarked on public-sector cutbacks that dissolved a number of public-sector agencies with a key role in rural areas such as the postal service, forestry, and energy, and either reintroduced them as state-owned corporations run on a fully commercial basis or sold them to the private sector.[60] Such policies create access problems because rural areas represent high-cost areas for the supply of primary services such as water, gas, and electricity.

In Australia, Smailes argues that both major national political parties agreed on policies that would directly affect rural areas – radical tariff reductions and radical cuts in government expenditures, which work against the interests of small family farmers. In the United States, Jacob, Bourke, and Luloff report that government tax support has declined for programs that are the primary conduit of mental health service delivery, especially in rural areas at a time when stress levels have become critical due to the crisis in agriculture. And in England, Bell and Cloke found that government deregulation of public transport had a significant impact on rural areas, resulting in a 'major polarisation between more profitable urban areas and the less attractive rural zones.'[61]

Many governments, in both the North and the South, have eliminated state-sponsored extension programs, in line with the dominant privatization agenda of corporate globalization. Denounced as economically unsustainable, public extension systems have been slashed through government cutbacks and structural adjustment programs, in spite of studies of privatized systems that 'demonstrate the negative effects of such systems, particularly on small farming.'[62] Originally set up for the purpose of improving the education of rural people, the demise of publicly funded extension programs is a harbinger of the assault on publicly funded education in general.

As employment in rural communities evaporates, government policy promotes a culture of enterprise to promote prosperity, but 'the bulk of those entering self-employment today struggle to survive, joining those whose work is poorly paid, insecure and often casual.'[63] This move towards so-called self-help has obvious distributional impacts for rural areas as communities pick up the functions that government no longer provides.[64]

Social Impacts

The impacts of corporate globalization reach far past the economic and political into the social lives of people in rural communities. Rural centres of agriculture, mining, fishing, and forestry are experiencing major social changes. These changes include decreased access to quality education, health care restructuring, declining social institutions, and destabilizing forms of migration into and out of rural communities.

Education is one of the sectors where the social impacts of corporate globalization are felt in rural communities. In many areas, small, rural schools are being closed and students are being consolidated in larger, urban and suburban schools. Driven by ideological considerations based on questionable claims of the cost-effectiveness of economies of scale, these closures ignore the superior pedagogical outcomes of small (rural) schools, especially for marginal and disabled students.[65] In addition, such closures overlook the vital role rural schools play in the web of community life.

In terms of health care, rural people experience lower levels of health than their urban counterparts. Research carried out in the United States shows that populations in rural areas generally suffer greater levels of disability, impairment, and mental and physical disorders than those in urban areas, while at the same time experiencing higher rates of poverty and less access to health and other human services. In spite of these findings, health care under corporate globalization is being restructured in ways that further weaken rural communities' access to essential health care services. In addition, health care restructuring gives little consideration to the role that hospitals play in the web of rural life. For example, in Ontario, rural hospitals are prime targets for government cutbacks without any consideration of the fact that the rural health care sector is not only concerned with health care access, but also with the economic, social, and environmental health and well-being of the community as a whole.[66]

The stresses brought on rural communities by the pressures of corporate globalization can affect the mental health of community members. Lorenz et al. report the continued impact of economic pressure on the psychological health of family members in rural areas. Jacob, Bourke, and Luloff describe how stress related to crises in agriculture in farm populations of the Midwestern United States was found to be correlated with incidents of depression, poor health, alcohol and drug abuse, domestic violence, and decreases in social well-being. In spite of these findings, there is a severe shortage of professional mental health support in rural areas, and a decline in tax support for this kind of service.[67]

The changes brought on by rural restructuring have also affected the viability of local social institutions such as churches, sports clubs, and social centres. For instance, by 1994 in western Australia, the majority of rural settlements that were not the administrative headquarters of local shires had not only collapsed commercially, but had also failed to retain any viable social institutions, which are so important to the survival of rural communities. Social unravelling was evident in Canada, where Ciccantell reports sharp increases in domestic violence and in alcohol and drug abuse, and less community involvement in three mining communities hard hit by rural restructuring.[68]

Cloke found varying social responses among rural communities in New Zealand that were facing what he calls 'the rural downturn.' While one community experienced an increase in cohesiveness and a feeling that survival depended on mutual help, another community abandoned the patronage of local services and facilities in favour of cheaper operations based in urban centres.[69]

In Canada, as in many other countries, the rural population is changing as a result of corporate globalization. People are migrating in and out of rural communities in response to the pressures of the global market. On the one hand, rural communities located within the urban shadow are experiencing the effects of *inmigration* as urban people move to the country. This phenomenon has resulted in an erosion of dynastic farming values because it makes farmers more likely to marry into and socialize with other social groups, and consequently are less prone to see themselves as a special group in society and eventually are less committed to family succession.[70]

Ward et al. report that inmigration has been associated with and helped to 'catalyze a major shift in public attitudes to agriculture and the countryside,' which has produced a growing gap between public perceptions of the function of the countryside and those of the farming community on questions of pesticide and land use. Salamon and Tornatore found that inmigration also resulted in tensions between local residents and newcomers with more wealth and education than established residents. They concluded that far from always rejuvenating rural communities, inmigration can hasten the death of a sense of community.[71]

On the other hand, rural communities located far from urban centres are not as attractive as areas for relocation. For example, there has been a general pattern of population decline in the western Australian wheatbelt, which conforms to national trends in comparable regions. Such *outmigration* is caused by the erosion of employment opportunities associated with rural restructuring, which produces 'negative multipliers resulting in the contraction of local economies, the withdrawal of services and further demographic decline.'[72] Thus, outmigration can start a vicious circle, which, again, can result in serious problems for rural communities.

Environmental Impacts

The economic policies of corporate globalization are having irreversible impacts on the environment. For example, policies such as comparative advantage increase the distance between producers and consumers, requiring the ecologically unsustainable transportation of commodities around the globe. Under the impact of increased economic activities, 'Our forests are overlogged, our agricultural lands overcropped, our grasslands overgrazed, our wetlands overdrained, our groundwaters overtapped, our seas overfished, and just about the whole terrestrial and marine environment overpolluted with chemical and radioactive poisons.'[73]

And while the wealthier members of society can afford to temporarily cocoon themselves from the environmental impacts of corporate globalization, the majority world is excluded from such a choice. Faced with an increasingly degraded environment, they must struggle daily with challenges to health and well-being that compromise their ability to 'compete' in the global market. For example, in mining communities in the mountain counties of eastern Kentucky, enormous wealth has been extracted by coal companies that have left the land wrecked and the people poor.[74]

In developing countries, the environmental impacts of corporate globalization include 'rainforest destruction, loss of biodiversity, desertification, land degradation, and rapid growth in greenhouse gas emissions.' While the blame is often placed on the low-income countries where such problems occur, it rightly belongs with the 'present consumption standards of the affluent throughout the world,' which are characteristic of corporate globalization.[75]

One example of the environmental impacts of corporate globalization involves fishing communities. The introduction of modern trawl fishing has resulted in 'gross overfishing,' driven by an ethic of 'maximum catch in the short run for maximum present revenue.' As a result, there has been a 'depletion of fishery resources,'[76] with devastating effects for those living in these communities.

Lumber communities provide another example of the environmental impacts of corporate globalization. Overlogging by transnational corporations (TNCs) has endangered both the forests and lumber communities, pitting rural residents against the environmental movement in a desperate attempt to save the last remaining forestry jobs. These residents 'frequently do not have the experience, education and expertise to speak to the issues on an equal footing. If they ally with their corporate employers, they are viewed as dupes of economic elites. If they speak for themselves, they are identified as victims, reactionary, materialistic, simply out of step with contemporary reality.'[77]

The intensification of agriculture under corporate globalization has introduced new environmental problems. Ward et al. contend that environmental problems in industrial agriculture have helped to erode public confidence, citing pesticide persistence, land-use questions and agricultural pollution as undermining the notion of farmers as guardians of the countryside. In addition, persistent debt has driven some farmers to destroy the environment they inhabit in order to survive. Some Ontario farmers have had to literally 'mine the soil' in an effort to produce ever more crops to pay back their loans. Barkin cites evidence of rural people in Latin America displaced to marginal lands by the pressures of corporate globalization, and having 'no choice but to devastate their own environments in the desperate struggle to survive.'[78]

Since agriculture is profoundly ecological as well as economical, global production decisions can have local biological effects: 'These are often environmentally destructive, but the farmers can seldom make changes to avoid such environmental damage without offending the market imperatives under which they work. No satisfactory mechanism is in place to change or overrule the market influence so that the local farming practices can be corrected. The necessary feed-back loops of economy and policy are missing. What we get instead are biological feedbacks of an unpleasant kind.'[79]

Under the money values of corporate globalization, the environment is reduced to a source and a sink to facilitate economic growth. The choice to use the environment in this way can result in the environmental degradation of rural communities. For example, Hildyard describes how the California Waste Management Board paid a Los Angeles consulting firm $500,000 (U.S.) to identify those communities that would be least likely to resist 'locally undesirable land use,' a euphemism for toxic waste dumps:

Such communities, according to the study, are characteristically rural, poor,
politically conservative, 'open to promises of economic benefits,' poorly

educated and already involved in 'natural exploitative occupations,' such as farming, ranching or mining. In effect, waste companies would be best advised to 'target' communities which in the consultant's view, are too stupid, too disorganised, too poor and too respectful of authority to resist the siting of dumps which would not be accepted in richer, better educated, 'professional' communities.[80]

Thus, under corporate globalization, it is clear that the exponential expansion of the economy is being accompanied by the accelerating degradation of the ecosphere – we are on a collision course with bio-physical reality.[81]

Gendered Impacts

Corporate globalization has had negative effects for women, not only in Canada but around the world. At the Beijing Conference for Women, the NGO Declaration stated: 'The globalization of the world's so-called 'market economies' is a root cause of the increasing feminization of poverty everywhere. This violates human rights and dignity, the integrity of our ecosystems and the environment, and poses serious threats to our health.'[82]

This feminization of poverty takes many forms. For example, the invisibility of women in global production is in large part a product of their relegation to informal sectors, shadow industries, homework, and other non-wage spheres of work. In addition, the emergence of a technical and financial elite has also brought forth a host of low-wage jobs to service the new economy, jobs disproportionately populated by women, visible minorities and new immigrants.[83]

Kerr summarizes the effects of corporate globalization on women by arguing that, in many cases, corporate globalization is 'undermining gender equality.' For example, in Africa, as governments shed their responsibility to provide adequate health care, education, public transport, or agricultural extension services, the onus for meeting those needs falls to women. In Bangladesh, women, not men, make up the cheap, flexible labour force to produce the export goods demanded by corporate globalization because they are considered to be 'more productive, submissive, and less likely to form unions demanding better wages, working and health conditions.' And in the Asian financial crisis of the late 1990s, women, who were among the first to lose their jobs, desperately sought employment in the informal sector, which 'has led in some countries to an overwhelming number of women and girls entering prostitution.'[84] Shiva echoes Kerr, describing the effects of corporate globalization on third-world women: 'The impact of globalization is ... to take resources and knowledge that have hitherto been under women's control, and the control of Third World communities to generate suste-nance and survival, and put them at the service of corporations engaged in global trade and commerce to generate profits.'[85]

In the United States, McMichael describes how the movement of manufacturing jobs from the United States to Mexico involves industries in which women are disproportionately employed, such as apparel, consumer electronics, and food processing. Once these jobs are elimi-nated, 'the possibility of regaining equivalent work lessens,' with a corre-sponding pressure on family livelihoods. Hessing concludes that the expansion and increased mobility of multinational corporations ... have contributed to the deterioration of the position of women.[86]

In China, young women from rural areas migrate to the coast and work in factories, sometimes from 7:30 a.m. to 2:30 a.m. every day for more than sixty days at a stretch. Such Dickensian conditions have led to what has been called 'over-work death,' when young workers collapse and die after working long hours, day after day.[87]

Tourism has been promoted in many rural communities after the collapse of traditional forms of employment caused by corporate global-ization. But the boosterism surrounding community tourism hides the division of labour often associated with it. For example, bed and break-fast operations mean that much of the menial work is done by women, work that is repetitive, dull, and without hope of advancement or skill development. In this way, tourism promotion can reinforce not only unequal power relations between men and women but also assumptions about women as caregivers. As Long and Kindon argue, rather than transforming cultural traditions (of which gender ideology is one), it would seem that tourism development is interacting with systems of gender ideology to strengthen and reinforce the status quo.[88]

The restructuring of many economies has meant that steady, well-paying manufacturing jobs have moved to areas with lower wages and fewer health and safety regulations. When these jobs disappear from a rural community, Leach and Winson found that women experienced greater wage decreases than men because of the nature of the jobs they were able to find after layoffs due to factory closures.[89]

In lumber communities, overlogging by forestry companies, and, in response, opposition by environmental groups, has placed some rural women in the complex position of supporting the logging industry against environmental initiatives to save the remaining old-growth forests. These women experienced a feeling of powerlessness as they 'saw themselves as part of a broader rural culture that had become disenfranchised from political protests and policy debates about environmental protection.'[90]

In farming communities, women work off the farm more and more to make ends meet. In New Zealand, Cloke found that farm women increasingly sought off-farm work,[91] which only added to their already heavy work loads.

Rural women's legal rights have not historically been the same as those of rural men. For example, until recently, Canadian law has 'elided from divorce settlements farm women's contribution to the reproduction of the family farm and the farm family.' However, such newly won legal rights are now at risk. Under the 'new right' agenda of corporate globalization, Bell and Cloke argue that the rights of women are seen as being anti-family, and are therefore exorcised wherever possible.[92]

Under the privatization imperatives of corporate globalization, the state no longer provides a growing number of social services. This situation often means that rural women must pick up the social services that the state has abandoned. In this way, the effects of privatization can fall most heavily on the shoulders of rural women.

Following the lead of feminist researchers, Argent discusses the active power of the gender order in rural communities. While some facets of the gender order are slower to change than others in the rural Australian area he studied, he found that it was undergoing an 'uneven but fundamental change.' However, that change is slowed by 'the rural media's role in constructing and perpetuating hegemonic discourses of rural masculinity and femininity (i.e., the gender order).' Argent sees such construction as part of the gender ideologies and identities that have propped up the Western rural idyll, an idyll that places rural women in a subordinate position to men.[93] With the commodification of the countryside ideal that accompanies corporate globalization, opposition to such ideology could be now stigmatized as 'bad for business.'

Cultural Impacts

Corporate globalization displaces the cultural legacies of countries around the world. As a replacement, it imposes a kind of mass culture that demands we come to see ourselves primarily as consumers. Consumption becomes a leisure pursuit, with going to the mall ranking second only to watching television, which itself primes viewers to join the mass culture of consumption. However, not everyone can partake in this mass culture. Along with the loss of welfare rights, both the rural and urban underclass have also lost many of their rights to consume, remaining 'unattractive clients' for the main corporate productive sectors.[94]

As corporate globalization penetrates every aspect of rural life, rural culture is being challenged by a global capitalist culture. Improved communications technology and globalization have undermined the distinctiveness of rural society, producing 'a more uniform social experience which is shaped increasingly by global trends which dilute the significance of local or regional ideologies and cultures.'[95]

Part of that rural culture is the main street of rural communities, centre of so much more than economic exchanges. With the arrival of big-box stores in rural communities, rural retail has been restructured,[96] and with it the main street atmosphere that formed the cultural backbone of rural life. Proponents of corporate globalization might argue that, in spite of the documented negative impacts of big-box stores, some rural communities are nevertheless falling over themselves to entice these corporate giants to relocate in their area. But this situation ignores the context and history that brought these communities to this sorry juncture. In his discussion of corporate hog farming, Qualman discusses the context that leads rural communities into such bleak choices. He asks, Why do rural communities lack investment capital and jobs? His answer takes us from the local to the global: the globalized, free-trade economy increasingly works to extract wealth from the areas where it is produced – often rural ones – and to propel that wealth to major urban financial centres where stockholders are clustered. In other words, in spite of the great wealth in many rural areas (e.g., grain, oil, cattle, lumber, coal), that wealth is not captured by those locations. Quite the opposite is happening: rural areas are struggling across the country. Faced with this huge outflow of wealth from rural areas, rural citizens and communities begin to see themselves as poor, and their local industries as unimportant. They misinterpret their situation and go looking for *outside* investment as a salvation – a strategy that is reinforced by every level of government. 'The mantra in rural Canada is that towns and villages need to attract outside investment in order to create jobs and save the community.' The irony is that much of this outside investment simply facilitates and accelerates the extraction of wealth and capital from rural areas.[97]

In many ways, in many countries around the world, the advent of corporate globalization has deeply altered rural ways of life. For example, in Europe, rural areas have become progressively less self-sufficient and self-contained, and ever more open to the wider forces – economic, social, political – shaping European life and indeed global development.[98]

Nelson fears that economic restructuring might undermine the exchange practices of neighbourliness that underpin the informal economy in rural communities, which has traditionally seen them through difficult times. Citing a recent study, she reports how many low-income residents in rural communities experiencing economic restructuring believed they could not count on most other members of their community for assistance during a crisis.[99]

Such findings undercut the very meaning of rurality, which is based on the notion that 'rural areas offer and foster distinctive cultures and ideologies and, therefore, a "way of life."' Increasingly, those ways of life are threatened as the impacts of corporate globalization are felt in rural communities. For example, in Canada, the ongoing farm crisis means that rural ways of life are at stake. Commenting on the survival of family farms and the towns and villages they support, one farmer asks: 'are we willing to let hundreds of communities fade away, taking their grain elevators, family stores and heritage with them?'[100]

Rural ways of life are incrementally giving way to 'lifestyles' that are based on individualism, consumption, and isolation, which are characteristic of the urban-centred experience of corporate globalization. Unlike ways of life, which are so deeply ingrained as to almost constitute a race memory, lifestyles are easily constructed and discarded. Among other things, lifestyles involve the purchase of commodities, which include 'both objects (cars, furniture, and so on) and experiences, such as holidays.'[101] Purchasing commodities to construct a lifestyle instead of living out a way of life buys into the culture of consumption that supports corporate globalization.

The economic, political, social, environmental, gendered, and cultural impacts of corporate globalization are clearly having devastating effects on rural communities, and the future of many of these communities is unclear. Wendell Berry goes so far as to suggest that 'since its inception, the industrial economy has systematically undermined rural

communities, and with globalisation, this process is accelerating throughout the world.'[102] In the age of globalization, how can we ensure the
sustainability of rural communities and increase both individual and
community well-being? An overview of research conducted during a
twenty-year period has given us an understanding of current conditions
in many rural communities. Now we need to build a utopian vision and
develop a strategy for getting there.

3 Strategies for Sustainability: Building a Theory for Practice

> Three essential ingredients can be distinguished in any effort to restructure current social reality: understanding of the existing society, a vision of the future, and a strategy for getting there.[1]

This book can be seen as an effort to restructure current social reality. The Introduction lays the groundwork for a vision of the future that is more inclusive than our current situation, and the first two chapters provide an understanding of the existing context in which rural communities are increasingly forced to operate. This chapter adds the third dimension to the search for sustainability: a strategy for getting to a future that ensures individual and community well-being. This strategy involves building a theoretical model based on three concepts: (1) hegemony, (2) communicative action, and (3) the life code of value and the money code of value. This model will not only be a useful tool for analysing current understandings of sustainability, but also will aid in building an alternative understanding of sustainability.

The future of many rural communities in Canada today is uncertain, given the impacts of corporate globalization experienced from coast to coast. Their sustainability is far from assured, and the possibility of a 'post-rural' world looms ahead of us. According to Immanuel Wallerstein, 'the deruralization of the world is on a fast upward curve. It has grown continuously over 500 years but most dramatically since 1945. It is quite possible to foresee that it will have largely disappeared in another 25 years.'[2]

Part of the strategy for avoiding the spectre of deruralization involves developing fresh perceptions and explanations with the help of a theoretical framework or model. Such a model can illuminate the problems rural communities face in the age of globalization and contribute to solutions to the current crisis in sustainability. Without a theoretical model, we may be unable to come to grips with the seemingly disparate breakdowns being experienced in rural communities: fishery closures, farm bankruptcies, soil depletion, plant shutdowns, groundwater contamination, logging standoffs, water shortages, and ghost towns. The importance of a theoretical model for analysing current social reality is emphasized by Lipsey, Ragan, and Courant: 'Theories are used to impose order on our observations, to explain how what we see is linked together. Without theories, there would be only a shapeless mass of observations.'[3]

Within the realm of human thought and action, theory plays a primary role, helping us to organize, understand and explain the world around us. According to Jürgen Habermas, 'The word "theory" has religious origins. The *theoros* was the representative sent by Greek cities to public celebrations. Through *theoria*, that is through looking on, he abandoned himself to the sacred events.'[4] Gregory also links theory to its Greek origins, maintaining that it connotes both openness and the reverent paying heed to phenomena.[5] While this heritage of openness and attentiveness has to some extent been lost in the struggles for legitimacy between theorists and practitioners, it still remains a goal to aim for when developing a theoretical model to help us deal with complex issues such as sustainability.

As a framework for analysis of social reality, theory can become a powerful tool in our understanding of sustainability and its relationship to the increased well-being of rural communities. In this way, theory can point the way to solutions – solutions that might not seem so apparent when viewed from the involvement of practice. In essence, a clear theory can be an engaging, transformative, and practical help to us as we grapple with questions concerning how to work, what things are worth doing, and how whatever we do fits into the work of others we admire, support, or emulate.[6]

A theoretical model acts like a lens through which we can look at the world. That lens may be distorted or clear, dark or rose-coloured, but it becomes a way of comprehending the inputs we constantly receive. While its view of the world may be partial, a theoretical model can also result in a blinding recognition of formerly incomprehensible aspects of the social reality in which we live. It thus becomes important to recognize its partiality while working with its explanatory power.

The Basis of the Theoretical Model

The theoretical model developed in this book will help to penetrate the confusion surrounding current understandings of sustainability and provide the basis for a new understanding of sustainability. It will draw on concepts from the work of three theorists: the concept of *hegemony* put forward by Antonio Gramsci, the concept of *communicative action* put forward by Jürgen Habermas, and the concepts of *the money code of value* and *the life code of value* put forward by John McMurtry. Sustainability, globalization, and the future of rural communities are extremely complex, interconnected issues that require a powerful theoretical model for understanding their dynamics. These concepts of hegemony, communicative action, and the money code of value and the life code of value will form the basis of a model that can help to explain the nature of these dynamics and enhance individual and community well-being.

Hegemony

Antonio Gramsci's concept of hegemony contributes to our understanding of the power of corporate globalization and the resistance to it that can help to build sustainability in rural communities. In his prison notebooks, Gramsci argued that hegemony comprises 'the "spontaneous" consent given by the great masses of the population to the general direction imposed on social life by the dominant fundamental group; this consent is "historically" caused by the prestige (and consequent confidence) which the dominant group enjoys because of its position and function in the world of production.'[7] While the term *hegemony* refers to the predominance of one state over others, and is close to one of the meanings of imperialism, twentieth-century Marxists such as Gramsci used it to denote the predominance of one social class over others, as in the term *bourgeois hegemony*.[8] This predominance was not based on consent alone. Gramsci understood that behind the spontaneous consent of the people stood enormous force, ready to rise up and protect ruling class predominance if consent failed to materialize or was eroded by experience: 'The apparatus of state coercive power ... "legally" enforces discipline on those groups who do not "consent" either actively or passively.'[9] 'Thus, for Gramsci, hegemony has two sides – it is characterised by the combination of force and consent, which balance each other reciprocally, without force predominating excessively over consent. Indeed, the attempt is always made to ensure that force will appear to be based on the consent of the majority, expressed by the so-called organs of public opinion – newspapers and associations – which, therefore, in certain situations, are artificially multiplied.'[10]

The spontaneous consent enjoyed by the dominant group and expressed in the organs of public opinion (such as the media, schools, and churches) results in a maintenance of the status quo that can be difficult to challenge because it captures the hearts and minds of ordinary people. According to Williams, 'Gramsci's most creative and distinctive development of Marxism, was his exploration of the *essential* problem of breaking the bourgeois hegemony over workers' minds, the need for workers and the workers' party to *think* themselves into *historical autonomy*, without which no permanent revolution is possible.'[11]

In exploring this essential problem, Gramsci came to understand that there could be what he called a 'crisis of hegemony' that could upset the predominance of the ruling group: 'the crisis of the ruling class's hegemony ... occurs either because the ruling class has failed in some major political undertaking for which it has requested, or forcibly extracted, the consent of the broad masses (war, for example), or because huge masses (especially of peasants and petit-bourgeois intellectuals) have passed suddenly from a state of political passivity to a certain activity, and put forward demands which taken together, albeit not organically formulated, add up to a revolution. A "crisis of authority" is spoken of: this is precisely the crisis of hegemony.'[12]

When it occurs, this crisis of hegemony is played out in a very specific arena – civil society – which both supports hegemony and provides opportunities for those who oppose it. Gramsci's understanding of civil society is very precise; for him it means 'the ensemble of organisms commonly called "private"' (as opposed to 'political society' or the state).[13] While some people romanticize the concept of civil society as 'the people' or 'the masses,' Gramsci's understanding of civil society allows for the inclusion of transnational corporations and the associations that support them. Such an understanding helps to explain how spontaneous consent to corporate globalization is cultivated and maintained in the minds of ordinary people. But just as civil society is a site of acquiescence and indoctrination into hegemonic values, it is also a site of struggle. Thus, in spite of the fact that people spontaneously consent to unsustainability, they can also oppose it, and in that opposition can learn to choose sustainable ways of thinking, feeling, and acting in the world.

Corporate globalization is a major hegemonic power in Canada (and around the world) today. The international trade agreements and government mandates that bolster corporate globalization give the appearance of consent, while thinly concealing enormous force.[14] This subtle exercise of control explains, for instance, why 'organs of public opinion' such as the mass media provide little other than corporate cheerleading masquerading as freedom of the press. Under such hegemonic circumstances, citizens have few opportunities for a wider understanding of global forces and tend to support the status quo, in spite of clear evidence that it is not in their best interests to do so. This situation may help to clarify, for example, why people in rural Ontario consistently supported Mike Harris's Conservative government, in spite of the fact that his policies threatened rural hospitals, eliminated rural schools, and reduced democracy through municipal amalgamation.

In spite of these circumstances, hegemony is always opposed. Occasions such as the meeting about the Multilateral Agreement on Investment in Paris in 1998 and the millennium round of the World Trade Organization in Seattle in 1999 provide openings or spaces for contesting hegemony through counter-hegemonic action, action that challenges the hegemony of the corporate agenda and reveals the 'consent' as undemocratic manipulation. Like saying that the emperor has no clothes, counter-hegemonic action can expose the elite interests that stand to benefit from corporate globalization.

Rural communities can also provide openings or spaces for contesting hegemony through counter-hegemonic action. As part of civil society, people living in rural communities can begin to address their sustainability through their resistance or opposition to corporate globalization. It is important to remember, however, that civil society is neither neutral nor value-free. It is dominated by institutions that support corporate globalization and is populated by those who maintain the status quo. Rural communities are no exception. Nonetheless, a kind of 'globalization from below' is rising around the world to counter the hegemonic power of corporate globalization. And one of the sites of struggle is rural communities, where people are withdrawing their spontaneous consent to the hegemonic domination of transnational corporations.

In this way, Gramsci's concept of hegemony will be an essential element in the formation of a theoretical model for analysing current concepts of sustainability and contributing to a new understanding of sustainability. The tension between hegemony and counter-hegemony highlights the importance of understanding and addressing structured power relations that can impede or enable sustainability in rural communities.

Communicative Action

Jürgen Habermas's concept of communicative action can offer a dialogical alternative to the monological imperatives of corporate globalization, as well as shed light on the global forces that are compromising the
sustainability of rural communities in Canada today.

A second-generation member of the Frankfurt School, Habermas
grounded his Critical Theory in a paradigm of language based on
dialogue. This dialogical move allowed him to posit a more complex
concept of rationality. This concept of rationality includes what Habermas
terms communicative rationality, which is process-oriented and based on
agreement, and instrumental rationality, which is ends-oriented and
based on domination. While instrumental rationality produces 'the
vision of an administered, totally reified world in which means-ends
rationality and domination are merged,' communicative rationality
'brings along with it the connotations of a noncoercively unifying,
consensus-building force of a discourse in which the participants overcome their at first subjectively biased views in favor of a rationally
motivated agreement.'[15]

Communicative rationality is contingent on whether or not participants agree that a claim is valid, not on its ability to exact control of the
world (like instrumental rationality). In other words, people oriented to
communicative rationality must raise at least three validity claims when-
ever they speak: that the statement is true, that the speech act is right
with respect to the existing normative context (e.g., grammatically correct), and that the intention of the speaker is meant as it is expressed.
Although raised and recognized in the here and now, and considered
'carriers of a context-bound everyday practice,' these universal validity
claims 'transcend any local context.'[16]

Linked to Habermas's two kinds of rationality are two modes of action
in the world. The first, based on instrumental rationality, is ends-
oriented action, involving either instrumental action to influence the
external world, or strategic action to influence other people; the second,
based on communicative rationality, is process-oriented action, involving
the attainment of ends through a process of reaching an agreement
based on mutual respect and understanding. The second mode of action
is what Habermas calls communicative action: 'The concept of communicative action refers to the interaction of at least two subjects capable of
speech and action who establish interpersonal relations [whether by
verbal or by extraverbal means]. The actors seek to reach an understand-

ing about the action situation and their plans of action in order to coordinate their actions by way of agreement.'[17]

Reaching an agreement must be uncoerced, otherwise at least one of the participants would be operating out of instrumental rationality, not communicative rationality. This uncoerced agreement depends on the 'unforced force of the better argument'[18] instead of instrumental force (such as violence or intimidation) that can 'persuade' people to 'agree' to a certain point of view, but only under coercion.

For Habermas, the process of reaching an understanding does not occur in a vacuum: 'Every process of reaching understanding takes place against the background of a culturally ingrained pre-understanding.'[19] That background of preunderstanding is a complementary concept to communicative action that Habermas refers to as the 'lifeworld': 'The lifeworld is the intuitively present, in this sense familiar and transparent, and at the same time vast and incalculable web of presuppositions that have to be satisfied if an actual utterance is to be at all meaningful, that is, valid *or* invalid.'[20]

Based in grammar, norms, and values, the lifeworld 'forms the horizon of processes of reaching understanding in which participants agree upon or discuss something in the one objective world, in their common social world or in a given subjective world.' For Habermas, these processes of reaching an understanding, or communicative action, take place within the lifeworld, which makes them interdependent: 'A circular process comes into play between the lifeworld as the resource from which communicative action draws, and the lifeworld as the product of this action.'[21]

Interpretation plays a large part in Habermas's concept of communicative action. While people's definitions of the situation can differ, 'in cooperative processes of interpretation no participant has a monopoly on correct interpretation.'[22] However, the task of interpretation is not without problems. In practice, Habermas admits that 'stability and absence of ambiguity are rather the exception in the communicative practice of everyday life. A more realistic picture is that drawn by ethnomethodologists – of a diffuse, fragile, continuously revised and only momentarily successful communication in which participants rely on problematic and unclarified presuppositions and feel their way from one occasional commonality to the next.'[23]

The lifeworld is engaged in a complicated and potentially destructive relationship with the system, the corelative of instrumental rationality. The system is made up of the economy, represented by the medium of money and the state, represented by the medium of power. A dialectical tension exists between the system and the lifeworld, which can have two results: either the system can come to serve the lifeworld or the lifeworld can come to serve the system. In the age of globalization, the latter case predominates.

One of the great strengths of Habermas's concept of communicative action is that it allows us to understand the effects of the system on the lifeworld and on the ability to arrive at mutual understanding: 'The rationalization of the lifeworld makes possible a kind of systemic integration that enters into competition with the integrating principle of reaching understanding and, under certain conditions, has a disintegrative effect on the lifeworld.'[24]

This disintegrative effect can become what Habermas calls 'the colonization of the lifeworld.'[25] In other words, the system of money and power can intrude on and take over the mechanisms of reaching mutual understanding, eliminating the opportunities for communicative action that both produce and reproduce the lifeworld. In this way, the colonization of the lifeworld can have negative consequences for both dialogue and cooperative planning.

In essence, the dialogical concept of communicative action can be understood as 'a conceptual scheme whereby one can diagnose pathologies of the "life-world" (such as its colonization by the system of money and power) and provide cures (for instance, an increase in communication, social participation, and discussion of values and norms to reconstruct society).'[26] Seen through the Habermasian lens, Canadian rural communities, like other communities around the world, are increasingly viewed instrumentally as potential sites of profit extraction for transnational corporations, not communicatively as places to live a meaningful life, raise a family, and contribute to building a more democratic society. Such instrumental rationality reduces all meanings of efficiency to economic efficiency and all meanings of accountability to the corporate bottom line.

Habermas's concept of the colonization of the lifeworld gives a name to the growing power of the system (i.e., corporate globalization) to occupy and control the human interaction that is so vital to mutual cooperation. As a result, the interaction that grounds communicative action to build the lifeworld in rural communities is being undermined by fear, despair, alienation, fragmentation, mistrust, and distraction. This situation compromises sustainability, and thus the prospect of increased well-being in rural communities. Habermas's concept of communicative action provides a way of highlighting the importance of dialogue to any understanding of sustainability, dialogue that is based on communicative rationality and aims to achieve consensus on the actions to take to achieve that sustainability. Such dialogue can counter the colonization of the lifeworld by creating opportunities for community members to participate in building their own sustainability.

In this way, Habermas's concept of communicative action will be an essential element in the formation of a theoretical model for analysing current understandings of sustainability and for constructing a new one. The tension between dialogical communication based on communicative rationality and monological communication based on instrumental rationality highlights the importance of understanding and addressing modes of communication that can impede or enable sustainability in rural communities.

The Life Code of Value and the Money Code of Value

John McMurtry's concepts of the life code of value and the money code of value add the dimension of values to the search for sustainability. McMurtry formulates the life code of value as the following sequence:

Life → Means of Life → More Life[27]

For McMurtry, *life* means 'organic movement, sentience and feeling, and thought.' *Means of life* refers to 'whatever enables life to be preserved or to extend its vital range on these three planes of being alive,' such as clean air, nutritious food, water, shelter, affective interaction, environmental space, and accessible learning conditions. Holding these capacities at their established scope reproduces life-value; widening or deepening them to a more comprehensive range increases life-value.[28]

In contrast, McMurtry formulates the money code of value as the following sequence:

Money → Commodity for Sale → More Money[29]

In this code of value, money is the beginning and the end of the sequence, because money, not life, is the 'regulating objective of thought and action.' In other words, 'the more money that returns to the investor of money, whatever may happen to life, the better the investment.'[30] Thus, money is not used for life, but life is used for money.

From this code of value, it follows that more money is always better by definition.

The life code of value expresses what McMurtry calls the 'life-ground,' which 'locates debate in concrete regions and ranges of people's lives, places in which the elements of everyday existence are deprived and people are terrorized by relations of power and the value system they express. By reconnecting values and normative inquiry to the disciplining base of the real world and, beneath that, its regulating values system, we re-enter the life-field in which received discourses of 'freedom' and 'democracy' are laundered out of sight.'[31]

McMurtry's conception of the life-ground is different from Habermas's conception of the lifeworld. While the latter is 'confined to the linguistic plane of existence' and means 'only the symbolic realm of life,' the former is 'much more comprehensive.' It includes all three planes of life: organic movement, sentience and feeling, and thought. A grounded life-sequence analysis 'keeps its eyes on life and its capabilities to think, feel or do, observing whether there is maintenance, growth or decline in these vital fields of being alive.'[32]

The 'instituted bearer' of the life code of value is what McMurtry calls the civil commons, which is 'society's organized and community-funded capacity of universally accessible resources to provide for the life preservation and growth of society's members and their environmental life-host.'[33] Inclusive rather than exclusive, the concept of the civil commons will play a major role in the search for sustainability and in the realization of the utopian vision of increased individual and community well-being.

An understanding of the life code of value and the money code of value has enormous consequences for the sustainability and well-being of rural communities. Depending on which value orientation is chosen (whether consciously or unconsciously), the outcomes will be very different. Choosing for life values emphasizes human and planetary life first and foremost – every other decision must be subsumed under, and conform to, this primary one. Choosing for money values emphasizes money accumulation first and foremost – every other decision must be subsumed under, and conform to, that primary one.

Understanding these value orientations helps to clarify how corporate globalization operates, and how it can be resisted. Based on the money code of value, corporate globalization puts profit maximization first and foremost, thus subsuming life itself under this guiding principle. Challenging such a money-first-no-matter-what value orientation must involve questioning this value orientation and exposing its limitations, especially those involving the destruction of human and planetary life.

Understanding these value orientations also helps to illuminate the grounds of the decision-making that is an integral part of sustainability, and thus the well-being, of rural communities. Sustainability based on the life code of value puts the reproduction or increase of life first and foremost, thus subsuming monetary accumulation under this guiding principle. Supporting such a value orientation must involve decisions that are clearly based on life values, without primary or unconscious deference to money values.

In this way, the concepts of the life code of value and the money code of value will be essential elements in the formation of a theoretical model for analysing current concepts of sustainability and contributing to the construction of a new understanding of sustainability. The tension between life values and money values highlights the importance of understanding and addressing value orientations that can impede or enable sustainability in rural communities.

Commonalities and Differences

These foundational concepts – hegemony, communicative action, and the life code of value and the money code of value – while substantially different, converge in some basic areas. First, they all include a dialectical component, which helps to highlight power relations that are often hidden or ignored by other theories. Powerful interests are at the core of our current unsustainable state, and these need to be exposed for analysis. Second, they allow a critique of capitalism, which is heavily implicated in unsustainable activities. The current global version of capitalism, with unregulated transnational corporations roaming the planet for sites of increasing profit extraction, is particularly unsustainable. Third, they permit an understanding of the role of ideology in maintaining our current unsustainable situation. Exposing ideology and breaking 'the *compulsion to believe* in the legitimacy of the repressive social institutions'[34] is a social learning experience that can contribute to an understanding of sustainability. Fourth, they allow for a utopian project, one that can provide a practical vision for rural communities. And fifth, they incorporate a place for human agency that is crucial to building a new understanding of sustainability.

However, these concepts also diverge in important aspects, and their differences allow them to complement one another in very forceful ways, opening to the creation of a theoretical model that incorporates the concepts taken from these three theorists: hegemony, communicative action, and codes of value.

Hegemony

Gramsci's concept of hegemony provides a succinct and useful way for understanding the predominance of corporate globalization and its seeming stranglehold on the hearts and minds of ordinary people. More forceful than Habermas's concept of the system, hegemony, according to Bullock, highlights 'not only the political and economic control exercised by the dominant class, but its success in projecting its own particular way of seeing the world, human and social relationships so that this is accepted as "common sense" and part of the natural order by those who are in fact subordinated to it.'[35]

While both Habermas and McMurtry eschew a framework based on class, Gramsci used a class analysis to explore the frustrating question of why many members of the working class consciously or unconsciously support the dominant class. This exploration resulted in the development of the complex and layered concept of hegemony, described in all its intricacies by Holub:

> Hegemony is a concept that helps us to understand not only the ways in which a predominant economic group coercively uses the state apparatuses of political society in the preservation of the status quo, but also how and where political society and, above all, civil society, with its institutions ranging from education, religion and the family to the microstructures of the practices of everyday life, contribute to the production of meaning and values which in turn produce, direct and maintain the 'spontaneous' consent of the various strata of society to that same status quo.[36]

Such an understanding allows us to see that opposition to corporate globalization cannot only come from key activists in society. In order to break the stranglehold of corporate globalization, the hearts and minds of ordinary people must be changed. This is a difficult obstacle, especially in rural communities, which are traditionally very conservative. However, another major difference between these three concepts can begin to address this difficulty: communicative action, and using dialogue based on communicative rationality to address questions of rural community sustainability.

Communicative Action

Habermas's concept of communicative action emphasizes communicative rationality and dialogue as the keys to reaching mutual understanding. Communicative rationality provides a co-operative orientation to communication, and dialogue based on the 'unforced force of the better argument' provides a processual aspect that is not included in either Gramsci or McMurtry's analysis of domination and how to overcome it.

Given our understanding of the insidious power of hegemony, we need an ongoing process of dialogical engagement that can begin to break the stranglehold of corporate globalization on the hearts and minds of ordinary people and build a willingness to work together to construct an alternative vision where sustainability, and individual and community well-being, rank first and foremost. However, the replacement of the existing hegemony requires painstaking and protracted political education.[37] Such political education entails more than communicative action. It entails a dimension that is missing in both Habermas's and Gramsci's theories: the dimension of values.

The Life Code of Value and the Money Code of Value

Politics has been described as the process in which a community confronts a series of great issues and chooses between opposing values.[38] In the way that Habermas's concept of communicative rationality represents a paradigm shift in understanding how people orient themselves to communication, McMurtry's concept of codes of value represents a paradigm shift in understanding how people come to make choices. Sweeping aside misplaced notions of inevitability or human nature, his codes of value explain how human thought, decision, and action are formed and carried out on a daily basis. Based on conscious or unconscious codes of value, these thoughts, decisions, and actions build stitch by stitch to create a matrix that can instantiate life values or money values.

Thus political education is essentially values education, an ongoing process of learning to choose between life values and money values. While learning to contest hegemony may be 'painstaking and protracted,' learning to choose life values over money values will help to replace the existing hegemony of corporate globalization with a more life-oriented alternative.

Together, these complementary concepts – hegemony, communicative action, and codes of value – will be essential elements in the formation of a theoretical model for analysing current concepts of sustainability and contributing to a new understanding of sustainability that can enhance the well-being of both individuals and communities. What will that theoretical model look like?

The Formation of the Theoretical Model

A theoretical model that incorporates the complementary concepts of hegemony, communicative action, and codes of value in its formation has three dimensions. The first dimension involves *structured power relations*, which would span a continuum between the poles of hegemony and counter-hegemony. This continuum between acceptance of and resistance to structured power relations sets up a range that runs from the spontaneous consent to structures of domination so vividly described by Gramsci, to the active withdrawal of that consent, which is characteristic of counter-hegemonic action.

An understanding of structured power relations is essential to any new conceptualization of sustainability in the age of globalization. Corporate globalization is a major hegemonic power in the world today, and without an understanding of how it works and what it entails, no conceptualization of sustainability will be able to challenge its hegemony through counter-hegemonic action. Any meaningful definition of sustainability includes the notion of struggle.[39] Counter-hegemony includes the struggle to break the power of corporate hegemony over people's minds and to help them think themselves into an historical autonomy free of corporate conditioning. In this way, counter-hegemony forms a necessary building block for a theoretical model that can analyse current understandings of sustainability and help to construct a new one.

The second dimension of this theoretical model involves *communication*, which would span a continuum between the poles of dialogue and monologue. This continuum between two-way communication and one-way communication sets up a range for communication that runs from communication that is community based, involves local stakeholders, and operates out of communicative rationality to communication that is based outside the community, does not involve local stakeholders, and operates out of instrumental rationality.

A number of authors who study sustainability point to the importance of dialogue. Robinson et al. call for 'increased public involvement in the development, interpretation and implementation of concepts of sustainability.' Sewell argues that if the decisions that begin the never-ending process of sustainability are made in the public realm, then the chance of getting those decisions right is enhanced.[40] Röling and Wagemakers also underline the importance of dialogue when they see sustainability as the outcome of the collective decision-making that arises from interaction among stakeholders.[41] In this way, dialogue forms a necessary building block for a theoretical model that can analyse current understandings of sustainability and help to construct a new one.

The third dimension of the theoretical model involves *values*, which would span a continuum between the poles of life values and money values. This continuum between values that place life first and foremost and values that place money first and foremost sets up a range that runs from values that reproduce or increase life to values that reproduce or increase money.

An understanding of values provides the underlying explanation for why people make the choices they do. Values undergird not only the choice between hegemonic and counter-hegemonic actions, but also the decisions arrived at through communicative action. Without an understanding of codes of value, we would be unable to explain, for example, how people could come together, and, through communicative action, agree to clear-cut all trees within a twenty-mile radius of their community. Without a life code of value to direct their decision-making, mutual agreement could contribute to environmental devastation. In this way, life values form a necessary building block for a theoretical model that can analyse current understandings of sustainability and help to construct a new one.

Each of the three dimensions involves a building block that can contribute to sustainability: counter-hegemony, dialogue, and life values. Together, these three building blocks form the groundwork for understanding sustainability. All three building blocks must be present in order to have a firm foundation on which to build. If any of the building blocks are missing, then the understanding will be flawed and ultimately unworkable.

Using the Theoretical Model

The theoretical model can be represented by a three-dimensional box, with the various box dimensions standing in for the three dimensions of the model (see Figure 1). The depth of the box represents the dimen-

Figure 1: Theoretical Model

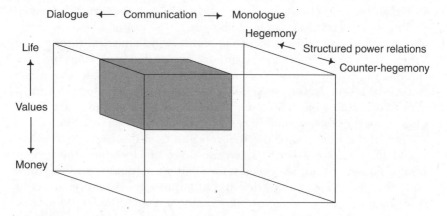

sion of structural power relations, with counter-hegemony at the front of the box and hegemony at the back. The width of the box represents the dimension of communication, with dialogue on the left side of the box and monologue on the right side of the box. The height of the box represents the dimension of values, with life values at the top of the box and money values at the bottom.

Within this three-dimensional box is another, smaller box, which represents the optimum area for grounding sustainability. Any formulation of sustainability that falls within this optimum area will provide a good basis for community sustainability because it will include all three of the basic building blocks. Any formulation of sustainability that falls outside of this optimum area will not provide a good basis for community sustainability because it will lack one or more of the basic building blocks. In this way, the three-dimensional model will allow for an analysis of current understandings of sustainability, and will contribute to the construction of a new understanding of sustainability. In terms of *analysis*, this theoretical model can assess the effectiveness of current understandings of sustainability by seeing where they fit within the three-dimensional parameters. If they lack one or more of the basic building blocks, they will neither fit into the optimum area nor provide a good basis for community sustainability. In terms of *construction*, this theoretical model can help to form the foundation on which to build a new understanding of sustainability. Providing the basic building blocks for grounding a new understanding of sustainability is the necessary first step to increased well-being for individuals and communities.

In the search for sustainability, this chapter has laid out a theoretical model that will become part of the strategy for restructuring our current reality. With this strategic model in place, we can now begin to look at current understandings of sustainability, pinpoint their strengths and shortcomings, and lay the groundwork for a new vision of sustainability.

4 Searching for Sustainability: Past and Present

The bounds of sustainability are set by the 'real world,' as well as our models.[1]

A popular term, *sustainability* has become one of those motherhood concepts that is hard to oppose, but difficult to pin down. Its very popularity hides the contradictions surrounding its use, hampering a clear understanding of the term. This chapter will expose these contradictions through an investigation of the idea of sustainability, its use as a concept, its history, and its definitions. These definitions will be analysed using the theoretical model to ascertain whether they can contribute to the search for sustainability.

Although the term *sustainable* has been in use in the English language since 1290, the word sustainability is fairly new, first appearing in English in 1972 and becoming more popular in the 1980s. Based on the verb *sustain*, it has its roots in the Latin word *sustinere*, meaning 'to hold up.' Gorman, Mehalik, and Werhane propose that 'to sustain something means to keep a phenomenon in existence, to prolong existence, to maintain, nourish, or encourage a phenomenon, and/or to strengthen or improve it.'[2]

While the verb *sustain* has a passive connotation and the adjective *sustainable* has an active connotation, the 'juxtaposition of both normative/active, and positive/passive meanings, has enabled the idea of sustainability to be employed in a variety of contradictory ways.'[3] The search for sustainability requires that we investigate these contradictory interpretations.

The Idea

The first set of contradictory interpretations involves trying to grasp some understanding of just what the idea of sustainability involves. The literature provides a rich and varied coverage of this problem. Some authors see sustainability as a goal or objective or end state – that is, some final point to be aimed for and arrived at.[4] In this sense, it is understood in both individual and common terms, and must be consciously chosen. Sustainability has also been described in the literature as a condition or a state that people are in or aspire towards, as well as a vision, such as a vision of economic stability or a clean environment, which can fill a void in the way we live our lives.[5] Some authors consider sustainability to be like an ethic, concerned with such issues as inter-generational equity, human survival, and morality, while others go so far as to see it almost like a religion, or at least a sacred cow.[6] In contrast, sustainability is understood by some simply as a management practice, without moral and ethical ramifications, or merely as a characteristic of some process or state.[7] From a more scientific perspective, sustainability has also been seen as both symbiosis and a manifestation of the second law of thermodynamics.[8] It has also been associated with systems thinking, and is considered by some to be an emergent property of certain kinds of systems, which adds a dynamic and unpredictable aspect to the idea of sustainability.[9] Some authors see sustainability as a principle that can unify people and guide choices, or as a form of mediation that can help to bridge the gulf between opposing groups.[10] It is also linked with the idea of a social construct – something socially constructed by humans for their own uses.[11] On a more philosophical level, sustainability is also seen in the literature as a 'metabelief,' which can open up whole new ways of thinking, feeling and acting in the world.[12] Sustainability has also been described as a catalyst for creative thinking, a liberating idea and a constant challenge to human ingenuity.[13] And finally, a number of authors see sustainability as a process, which means it involves an ongoing development or becoming without end.[14]

Rather than helping to clarify its meaning, these contradictory interpretations only serve to make the idea of sustainability more confusing. But they do indicate the kind of problem sustainability can pose, both in the literature and in the world.

The Concept

The second set of contradictory interpretations involves trying to understand what the concept means. Does it have a definable meaning and can it be of use in terms of policy and practice?

There is no doubt that the concept of sustainability has an important role to play, given our current unsustainable condition. Doob sums up its importance when he begins his book by stating:

> Sustainability: the concept appears as frequent references are being made to endangered species of plants and animals, to urban areas and forests, to pollution and the ozone layer, to economic development and political change, and to developing and developed countries. We may no longer dread the Cold War and nuclear warfare, yet many sensible, sensitive officials and the rest of us are alarmed by the ways in which environments and peoples are being treated. For the present era and the pending new century, therefore, solutions to these personal, national, and international challenges to sustainability are being vigorously sought or at least ostensibly expressed.[15]

There is some consensus in the literature that the concept of sustainability is linked to nature, both to the notions of husbandry, harvesting regimens, and resource management, and to the disciplines of biology and ecology. Notwithstanding its roots in nature, however, the concept often seems to have a decidedly human emphasis, reflecting not only a concern about our future, but also an unease with our current situation and an emphasis on human agency. For example, Siebenhüner posits *Homo sustinens* as a 'human being living according to the requirements of sustainability.'[16]

The concept of sustainability has evolved and diffused since its first usage over thirty years ago. Some people champion the concept, calling it 'the clarion of a new age' and 'the word of the decade.' Others are less enthusiastic, referring to it as 'hotly contested,' an 'infamous environmental buzzword,' and even 'treacherous.'

A number of people consider the concept to be vague. Indeed, O'Riordan has claimed that the concept of sustainability is 'deliberately vague ... so that endless streams of academics and diplomats could spend many comfortable hours trying to define it without success.' Buttel adds to this critique, describing how sustainability has been criticized not only for being vague, but also for being 'technocratic, mere rhetoric, inegalitarian, and for being a smokescreen for perpetuation of the status quo (neoliberalism, hegemony by the North).'[17]

Seemingly an infinitely flexible concept, sustainability presents us with a plethora of understandings, depending on the situation. Conjuring up different images to different people, its popularity should not imply that those who use the word agree on its meaning, or even know what it actually entails. Given this popularity, O'Riordan despairs that it may only be a matter of time before the metaphor of sustainability is so abused as to be meaningless. He goes on to argue that 'the concept of sustainability will probably languish as a "good idea" which cannot sensibly be put into practice – like "democracy" and "accountability."'[18]

On the other hand, Farrell and Hart disagree, arguing that although the concept means different things to different people, it is far from meaningless. They point out that the ongoing efforts of many organizations (ranging from local, grassroots initiatives to those of global institutions) are helping to change sustainability from a buzzword to a meaningful concept that is understandable to the lay public and that may become useful for decisionmaking.[19]

In spite of such optimism, the confusion surrounding the concept of sustainability has prompted some people to describe it only in negative terms, elaborating on what is not sustainable, instead of providing guidance on how to achieve sustainability. Kane highlights this shortcoming when she argues that 'we often go through a process of deciding what sustainability is *not.*'[20] Far from clarifying our understanding, negative conceptualizations only add to the confusion surrounding the concept.

As we proceed, it becomes even more obvious that the concept of sustainability remains very unclear. Contradictions abound in its conceptualization. Can a look at the short history of the term begin to clarify its meaning and help us in the search for sustainability?

The History

A modern term with an ancient pedigree, sustainability did not come into usage in the English language until the 1970s, but even its origins are confused. The *Oxford English Dictionary* records its first usage in 1972, when economist Thomas Sowell argued in his book, *Say's Law,* that an increase beyond limits of sustainability existing at any given time would lead only to reduced earnings and subsequent contraction of the quantity supplied. Contrary to the *OED,* Buttel describes how Adams argues that the notion of sustainability was inaugurated at the 1972 United Nations Conference on the Human Environment in Stockholm.[21]

The *OED* records the second occurrence of the term in 1980, in a speech given to the Royal Society of Arts by Lee Talbot, director of conservation for the World Wildlife Fund International. In his speech,

Talbot declared that 'clearly, sustainability in the management of both individual wild species and ecosystems such as rangelands and forests is critical to human welfare and indeed to human survival.'[22]

Sustainability emerged as a human response to the human destruction of the environment, at what Common calls 'the nexus between economic activity and the natural environment.' Before such destruction became unavoidably apparent, sustainability was not an explicit goal. But it was certainly an implicit goal: 'no human society has ever consciously promoted its own unsustainability.'[23]

As an implicit goal, O'Riordan proposes that the notion of sustainability probably appeared first in the Greek vision of *Ge*, or *Gaia*, as the Goddess of the Earth, the mother figure of natural replenishment. This original, simple formulation embodied the principles of adherence to natural laws and the evenhandedness of retribution. Redclift adds to the historical development of the concept when he maintains that 'the ideal of sustainability ... should properly be seen as the outcome of a quite specific set of events, beginning with the idea of progress, and associated with the Enlightenment in Western Europe.'[24]

The range and rate of human destruction, particularly in the twentieth century, has sparked a global debate about sustainability. A number of scholars see the Second World War as a turning point in the history of sustainability, but disagree about the specific cause: human conflict or damage caused by rapid economic growth following the war. Others see a different historical turning point, pinpointing the early 1970s but again disagreeing about the cause. While some contend that the sustainability debate was generated by the OPEC oil crisis, others maintain that the sustainability problem emerged in political and public arenas in 1972 with the publication of the book *The Limits to Growth*, and the United Nations Conference on the Human Environment in Stockholm in June of that same year.

The Limits to Growth was the product of the concern of an informal international organization called the Club of Rome, made up of scientists, educators, economists, humanists, industrialists, and national and international civil servants. While *The Limits to Growth* does not actually mention the word sustainability, it does highlight the dangers of exponential growth in a finite world, proposing a world system that is 'sustainable without sudden and uncontrollable collapse.' Using five factors that limit and determine growth – population, agricultural production, natural resources, industrial production, and pollution – the book modelled the consequences of equating growth with progress. The members of the Club of Rome concluded that the world needed to understand and prepare for a period of great transition – 'the transition from growth to global equilibrium,' a state in which 'population and capital are essentially stable, with the forces tending to increase or decrease them in a carefully controlled balance.'[25]

Common argues that although *The Limits to Growth* generated considerable debate and controversy, it had no discernible impact on government policies. Economists especially criticized it because of their 'strong attachment to the objective of economic growth,' an objective that they argued was the only feasible way to alleviate poverty. Not only did *The Limits to Growth* propose that economic growth in the world system had to cease if that system was not to collapse, but it also claimed that collapse was avoidable consistent with the satisfaction of the basic material needs of each person on earth. Such a claim implied a 'major redistribution of wealth and income from rich to poor as between, and within, nations,' which made the prospect of sustainability 'widely unappealing.'[26]

The Watershed: The Brundtland Report

The watershed in the sustainability debate was the Report of the World Commission on Environment and Development (WCED), commonly known as the Brundtland Report, after its chair, Gro Harlem Brundtland. Released in 1987 under the title *Our Common Future*, the report centred on the concept of *sustainable development* – development that meets the needs of the present without compromising the ability of future generations to meet their own. In essence, the members of the Commission saw sustainable development as 'a process of change in which the exploitation of resources, the direction of investments, the orientation of technological development, and institutional change are all in harmony and enhance both current and future potential to meet human needs and aspirations.'[27]

Sustainability and sustainable development were propelled to prominence by the Brundtland Report. It anointed the concept of sustainability, giving it a legitimacy and a currency that had eluded it for fifteen years. But like many subsequent publications, the Brundtland Report conflated the concept of sustainability with the concept of sustainable development, using them interchangeably in a confusing and contradictory fashion. Such conflation has only added to the current controversy surrounding the use of the concept. While the two terms are often used interchangeably in the literature, sustainability remains a distinct concept. Without a prior, clear understanding of the meaning of sustainability, compound terms such as sustainable development cannot be fully comprehended. The mother concept of sustainability determines the definition of any compound terms that depend on it.

In spite of this conflation, the Brundtland Report did raise both concepts into the realm of public acceptability, something *The Limits to Growth* was unable to accomplish. While the latter argued that economic growth needed to be curtailed if the earth was to survive, the former argued that 'Our report ... is not a prediction of ever increasing environmental decay, poverty, and hardship in an ever more polluted world among ever decreasing resources. We see instead the possibility for a new era of economic growth, one that must be based on policies that sustain and expand the environmental resource base. And we believe such growth to be absolutely essential to relieve the great poverty that is deepening in much of the developing world.'[28]

Thus, unlike *The Limits to Growth*, which advocated curtailing economic growth, the Brundtland Report did just the opposite by advocating increased economic growth as the way to reduce world poverty: 'Far from requiring the cessation of economic growth, it [sustainable development] recognizes that the problems of poverty and underdevelopment cannot be solved unless we have a new era of growth in which developing countries play a large role and reap large benefits.'[29]

In fact, in spite of worries about the future of the world's ecosystems and its natural resource base, the report does not contest the prediction that 'a five- to tenfold increase in world industrial output can be anticipated by the time world population stabilizes sometime in the next century.'[30] This affirmation of economic growth explains, to a large extent, the reason for the Brundtland Report's mainstream success, and the overwhelming acceptance of the concepts of sustainability and sustainable development. Indeed, 'the absence of any preclusion to continued economic growth in developed countries under the vision of sustainable development described in the World Commission report, may explain the ease with which sustainable development has become adopted by Western politicians and institutions of economic investment and resource allocation.'[31]

Seemingly a term for all people, sustainability was on its way to becoming a household word in a world looking for solutions to human and environmental crises, but becoming dominated by the money values of corporate globalization. Such overwhelming acceptance, however, should make us wary of the concept of sustainability, wary of the possibility of co-option. Lohmann, in his provocatively titled article 'Whose Common Future?' puts the issue in stark terms when he states, 'Never underestimate the ability of modern élites to work out ways of coming through a crisis with their power intact.' In the face of impending environmental crisis, Lohmann sees the more progressive global elites organizing themselves for the political management of the crisis by avoiding analysis of its causes, by using vague code words like 'security' to rally other members of the elite, by tailoring solutions not to the problems but to the interests of those who created them, by identifying the executors of the solution with the existing power structure, and by co-opting the NGOs to add credibility to their initiatives.[32]

Rees also speaks to the possibility of co-option when he cautions that the power of the growth paradigm is not to be underestimated: 'As sustainable development is gradually embraced by the political mainstream, its meaning drifts ever further from the ideal of ensuring a sustainable environment toward the seductive temptation of ensuring sustainable material growth.' He goes on to warn that carrying capacity is ultimately determined by the single vital resource or function in least supply. Such considerations 'call seriously to question the Brundtland Commission's route to sustainable development through a five- to tenfold increase in industrial activity. Indeed, it forces a reconsideration of the entire material growth ethic, the central pillar of industrial society.'[33]

Another criticism of the Brundtland Report involves the notion of substitution. Kane argues that the interpretation of sustainability in the report hinges on underlying assumptions of what is important for the continued existence and happiness of the human species, and the possibility for substitution of those things which contribute to our welfare. She provides a clear example of substitution in terms of the ecosystem: if people believed that future generations could meet their needs by inventing new technologies and reinventing or recreating ecosystems, then there would be no need to conserve any ecosystems; on the other hand, if we assume that technology and ecosystem services are not substitutable, then we should act to preserve as much of the biosphere as possible. By leaving the definition of sustainability open to interpretation, the report allows people to read in their own interpretations, and use it in their own interests.[34]

Since the Brundtland Report, the concept of sustainability has gained widespread acceptance, spawning such new terms as *sustainable livelihoods* and *sustainable rural communities*. But this acceptance has come at a price

– conceptual vagueness, fluidity, and co-option. That price is clearly seen in the Conference Board of Canada's advertising supplement in *Maclean's* magazine announcing that sustainability was a strategy of choice by the business community and touting the Dow Jones Sustainability Group Index as a good investment.[35] A long way from its roots in nature, sustainability in the age of globalization seems to have lost its moorings altogether.

The Definitions

The vagueness of the concept of sustainability and the confusion surrounding its usage not only spring from lack of a clear definition but also, in turn, pose problems when it comes to actually trying to define it. Jayasuriya sums up this situation when he argues: 'For a concept which has attained such lofty heights in current intellectual discourse and political debate, 'sustainability' is amazingly ill defined, or, rather, has acquired so many different definitions (and the number is increasing almost daily) that no one quite knows what is meant by the term.'[36]

The difficulty in defining sustainability results in a number of reactions, ranging from total reluctance to define the concept, to tentative attempts to grapple with it, to full-fledged definitions. A number of scholars argue that sustainability is simply impossible to define. For example, Farrell and Hart hold that 'no one group has the ultimate authority to define sustainability.'[37]

Another group of scholars, in contrast, believes that it is possible to define sustainability, but extremely difficult. In other words, few people actually define the term, but it is clear that a great deal of effort has gone into trying to do so. That effort, however, has not produced concrete results: 'The disagreements about the definition of sustainability ... reflect the conceptual problems associated with the formulation of a rigorous definition to describe a complex phenomenon, as well as fundamental differences in moral and ethical values. But a commonly accepted definition is essential if those participating in the discussions and debates are to communicate efficiently and meaningfully, and to ensure that the logical implications of specific viewpoints and arguments can be drawn with rigour.'[38]

There are also disagreements in the literature on how to go about the process of defining sustainability. For example, while Brown et al. divide their discussion of definitions into social, ecological, and economic sections, Köhn et al. are firm that 'sustainability cannot be split into economic, social or environmental categories.'[39]

In another vein, Röling and Wagemakers argue that sustainability should be defined by community stakeholders. Worster counters that 'national and international policy makers will want something more objective than that.' Richardson adds to this debate when he contends that along with the practical difficulties inherent in stakeholder definitions, such a choice 'deprives ... sustainability of any generic meaning and eliminates any basis for systematic evaluation and comparison.'[40]

The problems associated with defining sustainability have not stopped some scholars from making the attempt. The results vary widely. Kane informs us that since the Brundtland Report, sustainability has been defined variously as (1) maintaining intergenerational welfare, (2) maintaining the existence of the human species, (3) sustaining the productivity of economic systems, (4) maintaining biodiversity, and (5) maintaining evolutionary potential.[41]

Such a contradictory set of definitions provides a glimpse into the enormous variation of definitions found within the academic literature.

Perspectives and Definitions in the Academic Literature

The academic literature offers a range of definitions of sustainability, but provides few guidelines on how to choose between them. The various definitions tend to be dominated by a number of perspectives, which can roughly be divided into economic, social, and environmental. In reality, these perspectives sometimes overlap, producing hybrids like ecological economics. For the sake of explanation, however, the perspectives presented here are separated. Each perspective will be examined for its ability to fit within the optimum area of the theoretical model – the area containing the building blocks of life values, dialogue, and counter-hegemony.

The Economic Perspective

The economic perspective can be divided into two main groups: neoclassical economics and ecological economics. Overall, from an economic point of view, sustainability involves 'providing the typical person alive in the future with a standard of living, including both material *and* environmental welfare, at least as high as that enjoyed by the typical person today.'[42] The difference between the two groups involves the means for achieving this kind of sustainability. Neoclassical economists see the market as the means to achieving sustainability, while ecological economists also take the environment into consideration when describing sustainability.

Neoclassical Economics

Brown et al. note that an economic definition of sustainability is more 'elusive' than either social or environmental definitions because 'economists tend to assume the inevitability of economic growth and do not, for the most part, address the issue of sustainability.' Ultimately, however, neoclassical economists see sustainability as a constraint because 'sustainability definitions are mostly mathematical inequalities.'[43] See-ing it as a constraint has far-reaching implications when it comes to operationalizing sustainability.

When they directly address the issue of sustainability, neoclassical economists have their own definitions that are consistent with the neoliberal paradigm they work in. According to Worster, 'the field of economics ... has its own peculiar notion of what sustainability means. Economists focus on the point where societies achieve a critical take-off into long-term, continuous growth, investment, and profit in a market economy.'[44]

Under neoclassical economics, 'firms seek to maximize profits in order to plow them back into productive assets to increase output, sell more, and thus further increase profits, ad infinitum.' Given such an expansionist cycle, it is hardly surprising that a notion of sustainability that comes from a neoclassical economic analysis will 'involve a simple rule like maintaining the total capital stock at a level that will maintain consumption of goods and services far into the future.'[45]

Such a view of sustainability is seen in Kemp et al.'s definition of sustainability as 'meaning simply that consumption is kept above some subsistence minimum, so that life continues to exist.' This view is also reflected by the Conference Board of Canada, which sees sustainability as a 'strategy of choice' for Canadian corporations. Such a strategy, it claims, 'promotes a better bottom line,' resulting in 'long-term sustainable prosperity.'[46]

Sustainability is also seen by neoclassical economists in terms of utility. Pezzey defines sustainability as 'non-declining utility,' which he argues can be reduced to 'maintaining the capital stock intact.' He goes on to argue that any definition of sustainability that includes maintaining the capital stock intact must involve decisions about 'deciding how essential to, and substitutable in, production are the different components of capital: machines, technical know-how, renewable and non-renewable resources.'[47]

In terms of capital stock, neoclassical economists agree that sustainability is more or less assured in a well-functioning and properly regulated market system because they view natural capital and created capital as substitutes in production.[48] In other words, neoclassical economists, unlike ecological economists, believe in some level of substitutability when they define sustainability.

One of the biggest problems facing neoclassical economists dealing with definitions of sustainability is the fact that they have to resolve the limitations that a sustainable society must place on economic growth and need to deal with nonmarketable and often unquantifiable values of ecosystems and long-term global health.[49]

Looking through the lens of the theoretical model, definitions of sustainability from the perspective of neoclassical economics, when available, are based in money values, assume hegemonic power relations, and practise a monological form of communication.

In terms of values, neoclassical economics assumes 'the inevitability of economic growth,' which promotes money values first and foremost. Given this basic assumption, life is meant to serve that accumulation, and cannot be seen as a value in itself.

In terms of structured power relations, neoclassical economics assumes these relations because they allow for super accumulation instead of a more even distribution. It is thus no coincidence that in the cult of the individual, which is central to utility theory, there is no place for the collective or cooperative approach to life. Such an approach could increase the potential for social learning, and, in turn, the withdrawal of spontaneous consent upon which such hegemonic arrangements depend.

In terms of communication, again, there is nothing in neoclassical economics that questions monological communication. Indeed, it is clearly evidenced in the one-way economic policy forged in exclusive meetings, political policy created in back rooms, social policy dictated by bureaucrats, and environmental policy demanded by 'pragmatic considerations.' Such one-way communication is facilitated by the cult of the individual that precludes groups coming together to engage in participatory policy making. People in groups open up the potential for two-way communication, social learning, critique, and transformation, all of which could challenge the existing hegemonic arrangements.

In this way, from the perspective of neoclassical economics, definitions of sustainability include none of the basic building blocks, and thus do not fit into the optimum area delineated by the theoretical model.

Ecological Economics

A new branch of economics, ecological economics is not based in the neoclassical economic paradigm. In fact, ecological economics argues that conventional economic development models are responsible for, or at least aggravate, the sustainability crisis.[50]

Ecological economists believe that the economy is embedded in nature and 'begin their analysis with a pre-analytic view of the economy as a sub-system of the larger human society and institutions and of the still larger biophysical world.' This perspective broadens the economists' concept of value to include not only market prices but also unpriceable and even unquantifiable human cultural and environmental features. Such a broadening results in a definition of sustainability that involves 'handing down to future generations local and global ecosystems that largely resemble our own.' In terms of capital stock, ecological economists, unlike neoclassical economists, argue that 'natural and created capital are fundamentally complements – that is, they are used together in production and have low substitutability.'[51]

Looking through the lens of the theoretical model, definitions of sustainability from the perspective of ecological economics begin to address the building block of life values. However, they still assume hegemonic power relations and practise a monological form of communication.

In terms of values, definitions of sustainability in ecological economics move towards life values when they look beyond neoclassical economics to human cultural and environmental features. Instead of seeing the economy as pre-eminent, they see the economy as a subset of the larger human society and institutions and of the still larger biophysical world.

In terms of structured power relations, however, there is nothing in ecological economics that questions hegemonic power arrangements. Indeed, the idea of handing down to future generations local and global ecosystems that largely resemble our own does not necessarily entail changing the hegemonic power relations in any way, and can actually reinforce them, with the elite taking charge of the new global commons and 'protecting' it for their future exploitation.

In terms of communication, ecological economics does not question monological communication. There is no discussion of who gets to decide how to broaden 'the economists' concept of value.' Economists still dictate from on high – they just have a wider perspective.

In this way, from the perspective of ecological economics, definitions of sustainability exclude at least two of the basic building blocks, and thus do not fit into the optimum area delineated by the theoretical model.

The Social Perspective

The social perspective moves beyond economic parameters to consider human society as central to sustainability. In addition, the social perspective is often more concerned with individuals than with nations or the species.[52]

According to Worster, political and social scientists contribute to the sustainability debate by referring to 'the ability of institutions or ruling groups to generate enough public support to renew themselves and hold on to power.' From his point of view, 'sustainable societies are then simply those that are able to reproduce their political or social institutions.'[53]

Farrell and Hart provide what they call a working definition of sustainability, one which incorporates both social and environmental perspectives, when they see it as 'improving the quality of human life while living within the carrying capacity of supporting ecosystems.' Robinson et al. also provide a definition of sustainability that incorporates both the social and environmental perspectives: 'Sustainability is the persistence over an apparently indefinite future of certain necessary and desired characteristics of the socio-political system and its natural environment.' Another dual social and environmental perspective occurs in Redclift, who quotes Gordon Conway, president of the Rockefeller Foundation, as saying that sustainability (is) the ability to maintain productivity, whether of a field, farm, or nation, in the face of stress or shock.[54]

Brown et al. take a completely different approach, suggesting that a social definition of sustainability might include the continued satisfaction of basic human needs – food, water, shelter – as well as higher-level social and cultural necessities such as security, freedom, education, employment, and recreation.[55]

Looking through the lens of the theoretical model, definitions of sustainability from the social perspective also begin to address the building block of life values. However, they still assume hegemonic power relations and practise a monological form of communication.

In terms of values, definitions from the social perspective move towards life values when they look at 'improving the quality of human life,' 'basic human needs,' and 'higher-level social and cultural necessities.'

In terms of structured power relations, however, definitions from the social perspective seem drenched in hegemonic power relations when they talk about 'the ability of institutions or ruling groups to generate enough public support [i.e., spontaneous consent] to renew themselves and hold on to power.' Hegemonic power relations are further evidenced in statements that sustainability is the 'persistence over an apparently indefinite future of certain necessary and desired characteristics of the socio-political system.' Necessary and desirable for whom?

In terms of communication, definitions from the social perspective do not in any way preclude monological communication. For example, who gets to decide the 'higher-level social and cultural necessities'? There is no provision for the affected community to participate in such decisions.

In this way, definitions from the social perspective exclude at least two of the basic building blocks, and thus do not fit into the optimum area delineated by the theoretical model.

The Environmental Perspective

Environmentalists have their own definitions of sustainability, and the environmental literature widely implies that sustainability is essentially an ecological concept. The perspective of environmentalists bears little resemblance to those of classical economists or social scientists. The perspective of environmentalists centres, obviously, on the environment first and foremost, with a more long-term view of sustainability than the quarterly expectations of neoclassical economists.

The attitude of environmentalists towards economists regarding the issue of sustainability is summed up by Rees, who contends that 'there is no getting around the fact that material consumption is at the heart of the sustainability crisis.' Redclift takes this argument one step further when he asserts that 'modern economics has played a major role in the unsustainable development that characterizes North and South.' This view is reinforced by Buttel, who maintains that given the basically obligatory role of states in underwriting environmentally destructive private capital accumulation, ecological movements are essentially seen as the only significant agent of sustainability.[56]

Although overlaps between social and environmental perspectives on sustainability have been noted in the previous section, many environmentalists take a purely environmental perspective on the issue. For example, Drummond and Marsden quote a report by the British government agency English Nature as saying that sustainability is only concerned with the environment and has come to be an exclusively environmental term. In a narrow sense, it is related to the resilience of ecosystems (that is, their ability to withstand various types of stress), rather than any social or economic considerations. Brown et al. also put forward an ecosystem approach when discussing alternative perspectives on sustainability: 'The ecological definition of sustainability focuses on natural biological processes and the continued productivity and functioning of ecosystems. Long-term ecological sustainability requires the protection of genetic resources and the conservation of biological diversity ... In many cases, short-term natural variability is necessary for the long-term sustainability of the ecosystem.'[57]

Looking through the lens of the theoretical model, definitions of sustainability from the environmental perspective begin to address the building block of life values. In addition, they begin to address the building block of counter-hegemony. However, they still practise a monological form of communication.

In terms of values, definitions of sustainability from the environmental perspective move towards life values when they centre on the environment first and foremost. In addition, the recognition of the problem of material consumption and environmentally destructive private capital accumulation reinforces the move towards life values.

In terms of structured power relations, definitions of sustainability from the environmental perspective move towards counter-hegemony when they question private capital accumulation and modern economics. Such questioning opens up analysis and critique, which can undermine the spontaneous consent on which hegemonic power relations depend.

In terms of communication, however, the environmental perspective does not preclude monological communication. With the exception of explicitly participatory projects, such as Participatory Rural Appraisal (PRA),[58] there is little provision for bottom-up, community-based, stakeholder-centred input, which would, by necessity, involve two-way, dialogical communication.

In this way, definitions of sustainability from the environmental perspective exclude at least one of the basic building blocks, and thus do not fit into the optimum area delineated by the theoretical model.

This chapter has outlined a multiplicity of ideas, concepts, histories, perspectives, and definitions of sustainability. Confusing and varied, they do little to clarify our understanding of the term. Prugh, Costanza, and Daly describe the problem aptly when they maintain that 'sustainability is a big, sloppy term for a big, complex subject.'[59] Based in differing values, expertise, and language, these multiple views vie for legitimacy on the public stage and in the academic literature. The theoretical model has helped to analyse the current definitions, and found them to be lacking in one or more of the building blocks that form the optimum area. Given these deficiencies, it seems impossible to choose any of them, yet choices must be made in the very near future.

In the search for sustainability, our choices are rendered more crucial by the rise of corporate globalization, whose money-values logic seeps into every pore of our lives and insinuates itself into every decision we make. And while sustainability is clearly a more complex problem from the ecological perspective than it appears to be from the economic mainstream,[60] yet it is the economic mainstream that determines much of what we think and decide about sustainability. Given the ideological centrality of such a money-values orientation in Western countries like Canada, we could very well end up, as Worster has said, 'relying on utilitarian, economic, and anthropocentric definitions of sustainability ... Sustainability is, by and large, an economic concept on which economists are clear and ecologists are muddled. If you find that outcome unacceptable, as I do, then you must change the elementary terms of the discussion.'[61]

To 'change the elementary terms of the discussion,' we must begin to look at the problem of sustainability differently.

5 Searching for Sustainability: Future

Most discussions of sustainability focus on implementation and ignore the critical questions of what the world of our dreams would actually look, feel, and smell like. The trouble is, the sustainable world generally offered by environmentalists is based on 'restriction, prohibition, regulation and sacrifice ... Hardly anyone seems to envision a sustainable world that would be nice to live in.' This is a self-defeating lapse of imagination that could dim the prospects for achieving sustainability. There seem to be only two visions on the table. In the conventional vision, the human economy and population keep growing vigorously, and everyone eagerly chases the dream of greater consumption. The environmentalist point of view rightly denies the workability of this vision but offers in its place a kind of lifelong global celery diet. It is hardly surprising that most people choose the first path.[1]

This chapter changes the elementary terms of the discussion by putting another vision of sustainability on the table, one that involves neither greater consumption nor a lifelong global celery diet. Using the optimum area of the theoretical model as a springboard for a new understanding of sustainability, this vision will be founded on life values, dialogue, and a counter-hegemonic relationship to structures of power. This new understanding of sustainability, allied with the cooperative human construct of the civil commons, depends on feedback, evolves through negotiation, adapts to change, includes social learning, encompasses reflexivity, builds resilience, recognizes diversity, respects equity, encourages cooperation, and thrives in participatory democracy.

This chapter will lay out a new understanding of sustainability as involving *a set of structures and processes that build the civil commons*. It will begin by investigating what role structures, processes, and the civil commons play in the search for sustainability, concentrating on those aspects of the civil commons that are crucial to the realization of the utopian project. It will also deal with the idea of the commons itself, and the forces of enclosure that seek to overwhelm it. Finally, this chapter will explore what a new understanding of sustainability can mean in terms of resistance and an alternative vision.

In order for this vision to be realized, however, we need to know what sustainability can really mean. Parsing the new understanding of sustainability as involving a set of structures and processes that build the civil commons will help to clarify this meaning.

Sustainability as a Set of Structures

Structures have been defined as more or less embedded sets – patterns – of constraints and opportunities confronting decision-making agents, with 'institutions' simply being more formalized structures.[2] Structures can involve formalized structures, such as clubs, groups, associations, government, cooperatives, think tanks, and even corporations. Examples of formalized structures include the Council of Canadians, Women's Institutes, the Mennonite Central Committee, the Parkland Institute, and the Body Shop.[3] Structures can also involve less formalized structures, such as traditions and customs. Examples include cooperation, sharing, neighbourliness, and the largely forgotten concept of 'noblesse oblige,' that is, those with more being obliged to help those with less.

The constraints and opportunities that characterize structures frame the possibilities for sustainability. While *constraints* may be understood negatively, the word can also have a positive connotation. For example, a tradition such as women doing the bulk of child-rearing duties could be seen as a negative constraint restricting women's range of choices, but it could also result in the opportunity for local women to participate in planning a new neighbourhood daycare centre, instead of simply using outside experts.

Construing sustainability as involving a set of structures springs from the counter-hegemonic component of the theoretical model. Both hegemony and counter-hegemony involve relationships to structures of power. By actively withdrawing their spontaneous consent to structures of power, people can learn to build new, resistant, counter-hegemonic relationships to corporate globalization. They can also learn to build relationships to structures of cooperation and collaboration, thereby contributing to sustainability and to alternative forms of globalization. In rural communities, withdrawing spontaneous consent to structures of power can include a refusal to bow to competitive entrepreneurial pressures and an opening to marketing cooperatives, or a refusal to depend on the high-priced inputs of pesticide and fertilizer corporations and an opening to more organic ways of farming.

Sustainability as a Set of Processes

Processes have been defined as dynamic patterns of interaction and change that take place on or across structured fields of action.[4] Processes involve ongoing development and include learning, teaching, facilitating, researching, writing, governing, collaborating, and decision-making. Learning our way out of corporate globalization, teaching to transgress, and becoming involved in participatory democracy provide examples of the dynamic nature of processes.

Construing sustainability as involving a set of processes springs from the dialogical component of the theoretical model. Dialogue can be seen as an ongoing, two-way (or more) development with productive, reproductive, and transformative potential. It provides the interactional aspect for processes that build the civil commons.

A number of authors support the process dimension of sustainability. When discussing sustainable cities, Yanarella and Levine argue that sustainability can be made possible 'by placing it in a context within which it may be validated as a process.' Rasmussen also sees sustainability as 'a process with a beginning but no end.' John Sewell, former mayor of Toronto, concurs, describing sustainability as a process of small changes in the right direction – it is not an add-on, but an approach and a never-ending process. Sewell moves the idea of process into the sphere of dialogue by pointing out that decisions about the process of sustainability made by the public realm increase the chance of getting those decisions right. Röling and Wagemakers also emphasize this dialogical perspective in their book on sustainable agriculture by understanding sustainability as 'the outcome of the collective decision-making that arises from interaction.'[5]

This public process is not only a dialogical process, but also a learning process because it 'gives participants the opportunity to reexamine their beliefs, and the extent to which those beliefs may represent progress toward perceiving the truth more clearly, in light of the feedback provided by a community of others engaged in the same quest.'[6]

Such a process 'helps forge the *we* of community,'[7] which brings us back to the basis for the building block of dialogue – Habermas's concept of a communicative rationality that constructs the world in the communal terms of *we communicate, therefore we are*, not in the individualistic Cartesian terms of *I think, therefore I am.* In rural communities, this public learning process can be seen when a major employer closes down or moves away and residents engage in a community visioning process to plan for their collective future.

Sustainability as the Civil Commons

Seeing sustainability as involving the civil commons springs from the life-values component of the theoretical model. As discussed in the introduction to this volume, John McMurtry's concept of the civil commons is based on the life code of value. We now turn to an in-depth look at this fundamental concept.

What do the following items have in common?

• Universal health care
• Parks
• Public education
• Sidewalks
• The Canadian Broadcasting Corporation
• The Charter of Rights and Freedoms
• Old-age pensions

The answer is that they are all examples of the civil commons at work in Canadian rural and urban communities. As the instituted bearer of the life code of value, the civil commons is 'any co-operative human construction that protects and/or enables the universal access to life goods.'[8] According to McMurtry, 'The nature of the civil commons can be expressed as follows: *It is society's organized and community-funded capacity of universally accessible resources to provide for the life preservation and growth of society's members and their environmental life-host.* The civil commons is, in other words, what people ensure together as a society to protect and further life, as distinct from money aggregates.'[9]

Life-based and life-protective, the civil commons is oriented to life values, not money values. As such, it is a means to increased well-being and the realization of the utopian project. As a life-affirmative form of capacity-building, it builds the capacity of society to protect and/or enable universal access to life goods or means of life. McMurtry contends that there are two general kinds of means of life associated with the civil commons: '*protective life-means* (e.g., regulatory systems for clean air, water, food, and safe working conditions), and *enabling life-means* (e.g., universal education, public art and architecture and open environmental spaces).' The first kind involves binding social rules, and the second kind involves opening public spaces.[10]

A completely different frame of understanding from the priced consumption of the global market, the civil commons depends on universal accessibility, which means 'available without market price or other exclusionary fence to it, where need and choice concur with the common life interest served.'[11]

Like a race memory, the idea of the civil commons is embedded in our psyche. Developed over time and formalized in institutions like the welfare state, it represents an advance in civilization, reducing the possibility that life is merely nasty, brutish, and short. In this way, it 'defines a society's true level of life evolution.'[12] As McMurtry explains, 'Where there is an evolved civil commons sensibility, its concerns for fellow members of the community extend wider as it develops, past the family or the region to the nation and outwards to the civil commons of the world as it might be. The civil commons is an open possibility.'[13]

Examples of the civil commons include language itself, building regulations, water and power installations, bridges, social safety protections, laws, libraries, sewage systems, postal services, and social assistance. In rural communities, it includes marketing boards, producer cooperatives, benevolent societies, and guaranteed, affordable access to public services. In essence, the civil commons is 'the vast social fabric of unpriced goods, protecting and enabling life in a wide and deep seamless web of historical evolution that sustains society and civilization.'[14]

As such, the civil commons regulates in life-protective and life-enabling ways. While it has been built up over years of human existence, it can be dismantled very quickly by the unsustainable, life-blind choices of corporate globalization.

The Civil Commons and the State

At once ancient and up to date, the social construct of the civil commons has been brought to light as something that has evolved over time, but often below the level of consciousness. While some of it (like neighbourhood care teams for terminally ill people) remains informal, a great deal of it (like public education) has become codified and administered by the state:

> Government's collective functions have been won over many decades of social struggle against continuous criticism from market advocates to the effect that these functions are 'wasteful,' 'unaffordable,' or 'interferences in the free market.' For example, elected governments throughout the world have passed legislation to limit the hours of the working day and week; to establish safety standards and environmental regulations for factories and businesses; to permit employees to organize in workers' unions; to provide unemployment insurance and income security for those without jobs; to institute programs of health care available to all independent of their ability to pay; to provide universal public education and subsidized university education; and to construct publicly accessible transit systems, parks, and cultural centres free of cost or at below-cost prices.[15]

In this way, the civil commons is 'what any legitimate state or government properly supports,' and *what the corporate market will never provide.* Indeed, 'democratic government itself is the civil commons in one of its most powerful capacities of shared growth.' At its most developed stage, government 'becomes one with the civil commons, but is as yet far from achieving this full representation of the common interest.'[16]

In the age of globalization, however, the role of the state, and its relationship with the civil commons, is changing dramatically. Enabled by international trade agreements, the control of transnational corporations has become so great that they are surpassing the power of nation states. This growing control is having profound consequences for the civil commons, and thus for sustainability. According to McMurtry, the corporate system is structured to attack the shared base of people's lives – the civil commons – as a competitor against its program of profitable control of all of societies' means of life.[17]

Those who support the corporate system demand that government expenditures become accountable to the money code of value of corporate globalization, not the life code of value of the civil commons, with the following results:

1. The functions of government to protect and expand the money-code program of the market cost many times more than the entire civil commons.

2. Those who derive the money profits from these operations pay an ever smaller fraction of their costs.
3. These costs are increasingly paid for by defunding the civil commons.[18]

In this way, the state comes to serve more and more corporate interests and fewer and fewer life interests. In essence, the deregulation associated with corporate globalization includes re-regulation, with regulation involving not codes of conduct for business, but codes of conduct for states in which the latter are obliged to work to create favourable conditions for the former (e.g., NAFTA).[19] Such regulation leaves the civil commons crippled and vulnerable, resulting in a web of repercussions for the sustainability of rural communities as formerly public services are withdrawn from areas deemed 'unprofitable' by private service providers. In the age of globalization, people must learn to value the civil commons and fight for it. This fight includes maintaining the state's capability to support and protect it. That is why the agency aspect of sustainability is so important. It emphasizes that we can actively construct our sustainability – both formally through the state or informally through local community involvement – and that we can work to protect it.

The Civil Commons as Social Immune System

The regulating functions of the civil commons protect human and planetary life in deeply complex ways. McMurtry sees the civil commons as an immune system, fighting against invasion and breakdown, and providing benefits to the whole social body. These benefits include life-protective regulative recommendations, procedures, and penalty-backed laws to protect the health and prevent the disease of communities and their individual members by the multiplicity of harms, dangers, toxins, pathogens, and an army of negligent actions and practices that might endanger their survival or well-being. The social immune system can be summed up as 'that aspect of the contemporary civil commons whose function is to survey the social and environmental life-hosts continuously, recognize the not-self entrants or internal mutations which have no committed function to the sustainment of the life-host, and respond with effective means of selecting out the harmful substances or practices which endanger the life web of its members.'[20]

Like a bodily immune system, the social immune system of the civil commons springs into action in the face of threats to human and planetary life: 'Following the model of immune systems on the cellular level, we can observe that societies which have not been stripped of their social immune capabilities by the restructurings of global market operations have highly developed immune surveillance, recognition and response systems.'[21]

And like a bodily immune system, this defence allows the social body to thrive and realize its potential, not only within current generations, but also across future generations. As such, it protects the growth and development that is inherent in the ongoing project that is sustainability.

But like any immune system, the social immune system of the civil commons can break down, resulting in failure to recognize the appearance of threats. The greatest threat to the social immune system today is corporate globalization. It has the power to destroy the cooperative human construction of the civil commons, dismantling it in the never-ending drive to maximize outputs and minimize inputs. As such, it can destroy the sustainability project in all its aspects.

Those societies that have been stripped by the restructuring demanded by the global market agenda can be seen as having compromised social immune systems, unable to recognize the threats posed by corporate globalization and unable to defend humans and the environment against attacks by the global market. For example, the Conservative government of the Province of Ontario viewed regulations, which have been built up over decades to protect the public, as red tape, and instituted a Red Tape Commission to promote deregulation. In this climate of deregulation, the Ontario Ministry of Agriculture, Food and Rural Affairs promised to work with the Red Tape Commission to 'promote a positive investment climate in Ontario's agri-food sector.' But the social immune system of the civil commons is crucial for individual and community well-being. As Salutin asked, after the tainted water tragedy in the rural community of Walkerton: 'Does [Premier Harris] think all those rules, laws and agencies in public health and the environment – what you could call the apparatus and culture of the public interest – just fell off the turnip truck one day? ... They have a history and a reason.'[22]

The Civil Commons and the Environment

Rural communities offer a paradigmatic glimpse into the interface between human society and the environment, and thus can provide a working model for the civil commons in action. For just as the civil commons protects people and communities from life harm, the conscious human agency of the civil commons also works to prevent the destruction of the natural environment, the basis of all life on earth and the ultimate ground of human development. This agency ranges from 'environmental activism on the ground to international protocols to protect the ozone layer and emerging initiatives for environmental standards in international trade treaties.' [23]

Benton emphasizes the importance of our links to the natural environment when he argues that we are 'unavoidably organically embodied and ecologically embedded.'[24] This embodiment and embeddedness must undergird a new understanding of sustainability and help us to (re)build our relationship with the environment. In the age of globalization, intense competition results in the environment being used as a source and a sink to minimize inputs and maximize outputs.[25] As such, many rural communities become flashpoints of the destructive interaction between humans and the environment. In addition, economic policies like comparative advantage intensify the separation of consumers from the origins of the products they buy. For example, many who eat imported Canadian pork have no understanding of the environmental degradation rural communities experience because of intensive pig farming, and many who purchase Canadian lumber have no inkling of the local environmental repercussions of clear-cut operations.

The Canadian experience is replicated in countries around the world. David Harvey raises the issue of consumer alienation when he discusses the fetishism of commodities. Arguing that markets conceal social information and relations, he adds that 'We cannot tell from looking at the commodity whether it has been produced by happy laborers working in a cooperative in Italy, grossly exploited laborers working under conditions of apartheid in South Africa, or wage laborers protected by adequate labor legislation and wage agreements in Sweden. The grapes that sit upon the supermarket shelves are mute; we cannot see the fingerprints of exploitation upon them or tell immediately what part of the world they are from.'[26]

To Harvey's argument about social exploitation we can add the dimension of environmental exploitation. Markets also conceal environmental information and relations. We cannot tell from looking at most commodities whether they have been produced in an environmentally friendly fashion or whether their production involved habitat destruction, soil degradation, or groundwater contamination.[27]

On many levels, the natural environment has become an externality, not only for transnational corporations, but also for individuals and communities. We have become distanced and alienated from the very basis of life. According to Lauzon, the environmental crisis is a consequence of our alienated condition – industrialization and the primacy of the free market economy have both shaped our interpersonal relationships and increasingly isolated us from the planet itself. As a result, some people 'look to the natural world and see values, investments and potential profits rather than divine epiphanies.' Proposing that we look for new ways of knowing to counter this objective knowing, which eventually leads to an ecologically disastrous way of knowing, he advocates that 'we need to surrender our species chauvinism ... and develop our capacity for empathetic knowledge, knowledge so that we may have the insight that allows us to cooperate with nature and find our security in belonging to a community.'[28]

Such empathetic ways of knowing need to be woven into a new understanding of sustainability if we are to survive as a species. Based in the utopian project, they can help to foster the kind of relationship with the environment that stresses the interconnectedness of all things. Ultimately, we must come to know what the Buddha said in his first sermon: Everything depends in its origination on everything else at once and in unison.[29]

A wide spectrum of thinkers has not recognized this interconnection. On the contrary, McMurtry points out, in the dominant conception of the environment, non-human nature is of value only so far as it can be used instrumentally for human purposes, not as a value in its own right. In the face of clear evidence of environmental breakdown, however, such 'ecocidal' thinking is gradually being replaced by a new realization: the general fact is that human and environmental life sequences are linked so that people's health depends on the health of their environments.[30] Nowhere is this clearer than in the rural community of Walkerton, where instrumental thinking about the environment on many levels resulted in many people dying and hundreds more becoming ill because of E-coli bacteria in the community water system.

This general fact of our interrelatedness, and embeddedness, means that the civil commons encompasses the idea that if the natural environment is threatened, so is human life. But in a telling reversal from the human situation, it is not what we *do* to the environment, but what we *don't do*: 'The way in which humans can sustain their environmental life-host, then, is not by providing for *its* means of life, for this is not required or possible. The only way in which 'sustainability' of the environmental life-sequence can be achieved is by humans *not systemically depleting, polluting, or destroying* it. It takes care of its own life-sequence in the macrocosm and of an infinitude of sub-sequences at the same time with no interference needed.'[31]

The money values of corporate globalization, however, are an evolving threat to the natural environment, and therefore to human existence, because they presuppose the environment as a source and a sink in the endless quest for ever higher profits. For example, a recent survey, conducted by the United Nations, of 794 leading transnational corporations with sales over $1 billion (U.S.) per annum showed that most large companies attach relatively little importance to any environmental considerations likely to reduce their profitability.[32] This lack of consideration for the environment has serious implications for rural communities as natural resources are withdrawn at increasing rates and the noxious by-products of the industrial economy are dumped in rural areas in order to better the corporate bottom line.

Driven by the money code of value, the economic growth imperative has often overridden environmental viability, as in the 'environmentally disruptive growth' in Europe during the postwar period of 1945 to 1975. Such growth can also be seen in the ecological degradation that accompanies industrialized agriculture, which needs to 'continually expand production to maintain profits,' decreasing environmental viability as it increases shareholder value. The environmental effects of the growth imperative can be seen as well in the so-called 'Tiger' economies of East Asia, where 'air pollution in cities is growing faster than the rate of economic growth.' These examples highlight what Brecher, Costello, and Smith label as the 'environmental race to the bottom.' This race is exacerbated by international trade agreements, which enshrine money values in a growing body of case law. For instance, under the proposed Free Trade Area of the Americas (FTAA), all future Canadian federal and provincial environmental and natural resource protection regulations must be vetted by the Department of Foreign Affairs and International Trade (DFAIT) to make sure they do not infringe upon corporate rights.[33]

Sustainability would not even be an issue without human destruction of the environment,[34] especially the kind of destruction carried out in the name of the economic efficiency demanded by the mature form of capitalism known as corporate globalization. In fact, 'the global market system can be seen to be carcinogenic in its pattern to the extent that it strips, as it does now, the evolving civil commons of its effective means of environmental protection.'[35]

A clear example of stripping the civil commons of its effective means of environmental protection can be seen in the actions of the Conservative government in Ontario. The Canadian Environmental Law Association has documented these actions. For example,

- The government has made crippling cuts to the budgets of the Ministry of the Environment, Conservation Authorities, and the Ministry of Natural Resources, leaving them unable to enforce environmental regulations.
- The government has loaded municipalities with environmental responsibilities, while at the same time tying their hands by withdrawing funding to carry out these responsibilities.
- The government considers environmental protection as red tape, so calls for deregulation, or the dismantling, of environmental regulations.
- The government's new environmental protection laws are weak, and its focus on enforcement is ineffective, inefficient, and expensive.
- The government has opened up formerly protected areas by guaranteeing access by forestry and mining industries under its 'Lands for Life' [sic] process.[36]

These government actions can have serious repercussions for rural communities, which often experience the impacts of environmental degradation in immediate and visceral ways. But just as decisions based on the money code of value can wreak havoc on the environment, decisions based on the life code of value can protect it. Indeed, the civil commons is 'the sole protector of society's environmental life-host,'[37] so any attack on the civil commons is an attack on global life itself. A large number of people are working to stave off such attacks, challenging the deregulating, privatizing agenda of corporate globalization, or globalization from above.

The Civil Commons and Globalization from Below

A worldwide movement of resistance, globalization from below has now established itself as a global opposition, representing the interests of people and the environment.[38] The life interests of the civil commons form the basis of this global opposition, the common ground that loosely unifies the numerous groups involved in globalization from below.

When discussing the opposition to corporate globalization, McMurtry argues that: 'Those whose lives and communities are directly assaulted by the system's invasions ... declare that a war is being waged against their very existence, and they rise up against it. The battle is being waged across the globe, and it is everywhere against the assault on life and the civil commons by the money-sequence in its multiple forms.'[39]

Globalization from below is fundamentally opposed to the money-sequence of value. Opposition rises up from below in many forms, such as community activism, street demonstrations, information sessions, horizontal alliances, alternative media, and grassroots networking. Dialogical, counter-hegemonic and life affirming, globalization from below presents a growing challenge to globalization from above:

> Like a slow brush fire across the globe, ever more people feel what is happening, sense the pattern that is unfolding, intuit the urgency to restore the life-code to rule. They have begun to join for and across the civil commons of the world as an emergent ground of shared life and agency – through government for the common interest and against government for corporate administration, outside the institutions of oppression but storming them for instituted rules to protect life. It is coming up from the ground. The ancient vocation of protecting the common life-interest is at work within and across the most apparently disparate intentions. It is in defence of life and the civil commons across struggles. It is demanding government for the commonweal beyond bureaucratic evasion and opportunism. And it is beginning to lay bare the closed corporate money-sequence that invades all of life to turn it into itself. The uniting of the servants of life's freedom is as old as historical movements, but never more challenged than now. Assistance to the hungry, the homeless, the poor, and the powerless is as ancient as human vision, but has never been more equipped than at the present. It is no exaggeration to say that we are at a turning point in the world's history.[40]

Rural communities play an active role in globalization from below. Farmers' protests against genetically modified organisms, fishers' demonstrations against factory trawlers, and community members fighting offshore tourism schemes, big box stores, and urban garbage all form part of the vast web of the grassroots challenge to globalization from above.

The Civil Commons in Rural Communities

In the age of globalization, rural communities in particular find them-selves at a turning point in history. Challenged like never before by the impacts of corporate globalization, many are struggling to survive in the twenty-first century. Ultimately, the difficulty of envisioning an alternative future for rural communities is surpassed by the necessity of doing so.[41] To avoid becoming toxic waste sites, ghost towns, or tourist muse-ums, rural communities need to clearly recognize the challenges they face, find their civil commons bearings, and build an alternative to corporate globalization.

The civil commons in rural communities takes on many different forms, from municipal bylaws to community customs. The following are just a few examples of the civil commons in rural communities in Canada:

- Rural post offices
- Rural schools
- Marketing boards
- Rural hospitals
- Farmers' markets
- Barn raisings
- the Crow rate[42]

Although universal in certain respects, the civil commons is also pro-foundly local, capable of addressing crucial rural concerns such as water quality, primary resource use, and access to services. It works on micro, meso, and macro levels, from individual to global considerations. Oper-ating on a range of scales, the civil commons is a vehicle to address a wide spectrum of life issues, from a community playground project to global human rights. It is, in essence, 'the living bonds of community organized to transform the life of all its citizens to a more comprehen-sive, vital being.'[43]

Community economic development can be one of the sources of local sustainability if it involves the civil commons. Rural community develop-ment has traditionally centred on job creation, at all costs. In his book *Broken Heartland: The Rise of America's Rural Ghettos* Davidson explains how job-centred economic development sets communities, states, and whole regions against each other in a destructive competition to attract jobs by giving up more and more of themselves economically, environ-

mentally, and socially. In contrast to this narrowly constructed understanding of development that simply reinforces the cycle of decline it is
designed to end, Davidson argues for a form of community development
that takes into account economic, environmental, and social factors,
which together determine the quality of life enjoyed by residents.[44]
Taking Davidson's argument one step further, we can propose a more
holistic approach to community economic development, one centred
on building and enhancing the civil commons in its economic, environmental, and social aspects. Consistent with Davidson's vision of rural
residents' quality of life, this new understanding of community economic development would promote increased individual and community well-being – the goal of sustainability.

The Civil Commons and the Traditional Commons

McMurtry is careful to distinguish between the traditional commons and
his concept of the civil commons:

> I have introduced the concept of 'civil commons' to distinguish it from the
> traditional 'commons' – the shared natural lands upon which an agricul-
> tural village economy depends. I mean by the civil commons both the
> traditional commons and all other universally accessible goods of life that
> protect or enable the lives of society's members ... the concept of the civil
> commons subsumes both the traditional commons and the built commons
> of universally accessible social goods evolved by public sectors since the
> Industrial Revolution and, in particular, since the end of World War II.[45]

This distinction is crucial to our understanding of the role of the civil
commons. McMurtry emphasizes that it is important to distinguish between 'the commons' as nature-given land or resource and 'the civil
commons' which effectively protects it, and ensures access of all members
of the community to its continuing means of existence. In this way, the
civil commons is 'civil' insofar as the common life good it embodies is
protected by *conscious and co-operative human agency*.[46] As long-standing sites
of common land or resources, rural communities around the world have
been at the centre of civil commons protections for hundreds of years.

But just as the traditional commons were cleared by acts of enclosure
to make way for private profit, so too the civil commons is currently
being cleared by the policies of corporate globalization to make way for
private profit. There is now no place in the world, rural or urban, in

which the civil commons is safe from the invasion of the money code of value. The roots of this enclosure of the civil commons lie in an understanding that has been formed about the traditional commons, which is encapsulated in the phrase 'the tragedy of the commons.'

Whose Tragedy of the Commons?

In 1968, Garrett Hardin, a professor of biology, wrote an article entitled 'The Tragedy of the Commons' in which he argued that the commons could not work as a concept because of human greed. After projecting the self-maximizing principle of neoclassical economics onto others who do not operate out of that value system, he advocated that 'the tragedy of the commons as a food basket is averted by private property, or something formally like it.'[47]

Hardin's work has been critiqued from a number of quarters. Niels Röling has argued that Hardin was wrong in his understanding of the commons because he did not distinguish between the commons and an open-access resource. According to Röling, the corporate market is an open-access resource, or makes things that way, but people can create areas where they agree on another way of dealing with resources.[48]

Maria Mies and Veronica Bennholdt-Thomsen have also critiqued Hardin. Before concluding that Hardin's arguments contain in a nutshell all the ideology and justification of globalization, liberalization, and privatization, they discuss the new, emerging discourse of the 'global commons': 'there are two different, opposite concepts of "reinventing the commons": first ours, which means to defend, to reclaim and to reinvent the commons from below, through grassroots action of local people for local people; and second, the concept constructed and invented from above, namely the concept of "global commons," which is being introduced by international agencies and global players, mostly for the benefit of TNCs [transnational corporations].'[49]

And an interdisciplinary team of researchers has argued that, given the fact that a 'surprising number of cases exist in which users have been able to restrict access to the resource and establish rules among themselves for its sustainable use,' therefore a 'more complete theory than Hardin's should incorporate institutional arrangements and cultural factors to provide better analysis and prediction.'[50]

Hardin's so-called tragedy of the commons is thus shown to be a tragedy only in the eyes of those who stand to benefit from the privatization of common property. The real tragedy, for them, is that they cannot make a profit from these common resources. And just as there has been a history of relentless expropriation of the traditional commons around the world, there is now an ongoing expropriation of the civil commons for private gain through the privatization of explicitly public goods.

From the Enclosure of the Commons to the Assault on the Civil Commons

As we gain an understanding of the civil commons and its role in the history of human civilization, we also begin to understand how it is built and how it is destroyed. Its destruction is not the inevitable outcome of human greed, but the careful orchestration of media campaigns, policy decisions, and political capitulations to global corporate pressure. We have not 'lived beyond our means,' as we have been so often told, but are being swindled out of our human birthright by those who would benefit from the privatization of the civil commons. Corporate globalization is everywhere working to destroy the civil commons so that everyone will be dependent not on the unpriced goods of the civil commons, but on the priced goods of the global market. How will a new understanding of sustainability help to prevent a modern enclosure of the commons and open the way for the realization of increased well-being in rural communities?

A New Understanding of Sustainability

Sustainability involves a set of structures and processes that build the civil commons. The concept of the civil commons gives a name to the cooperative human agency that has sustained us in many forms over millennia. The structures and processes form a dialectical dynamic that contributes to the civil commons through the synthesis of their interactions. Together, they work to provide universal access to life goods on a multi-scalar front.

The role of a new understanding of sustainability will be to support resistance to corporate globalization's escalating enclosure of the civil commons and to provide alternative visions to the dystopia of the exclusion of the global market. This two-pronged approach allows a new understanding of sustainability to play not only a problem-solving role, but also a creative role. Both roles are crucial to the utopian project.

Resistance

In conjunction with the impacts of corporate globalization comes resistance to it. Far from united, this resistance takes many forms at the local, national, and international levels. Resistance, however, is not without problems. In the community and in the workplace, a number of difficulties are associated with resistance:

1. There is a danger that resistance will fall into the trap of fundamentalism, of being reactive, and ultimately of being reactionary.
2. Since most resistance is local, there is a constant danger that it will be co-opted or manipulated.
3. Resistance often remains somewhat localized, isolated, and fragmented.
4. Resistance tends to be fragmented around issues – resistance against cultural practices, against ecological destruction, or against economic marginalisation – without much linkage. Such fragmentation makes it difficult for learning our way out in a coordinated and coherent way.[51]

In addition, the more developed a society, the more disconnected people's lives will be from what their resistance actually aspires to, and this distance is more or less proportional to the degree of institutionalization.[52]

What do these difficulties mean for Canadian rural communities struggling under the impacts of corporate globalization? Would resistance be futile, as the neoliberal ideology of inevitability suggests? By no means. Fundamentalism, co-option, and fragmentation, though clear and present dangers, are not insurmountable obstacles. For example, as McHattie paints out, farmers in India, though widely varied and dispersed, have united against the marketing practices of the corporate giant, Monsanto.[53] While Canadian rural communities are part of a highly industrialized society, they still retain connections with the environment, with primary industries and crafts, and with relatively (or recently) intact social structures. This 'rural advantage' moves them closer to the alternatives they envision. According to Finger and Asún, these alternatives generally relate to sustainable communities, which they see as grounded in resistance from the bottom up. And it is this resistance that 'gives people the energy and the motivation to develop alternatives.'[54] What could these alternative visions look like?

Alternative Visions

If sustainability is understood as involving a set of structures and processes that build the civil commons, then what would a sustainable world actually look, feel, and smell like? How would we know we were on the right path? Could we build alternative visions that would not require a 'lifelong global celery diet,' but would be 'nice to live in'? Allman lays out what it means to build a vision: 'If we are going to create a more humanized form of existence, we need at least a broad notion of what this would entail. Any vision worth striving for must be realistic rather than whimsical. It must be based on considerations and critiques of the past and present human condition. In other words, to be achievable, a vision must be derived from the real, the material world.'[55]

The vision of sustainability developed in this book is based in the real world of the civil commons. This vision stands in opposition to the 'Market as God' promoted by those who believe in corporate globalization.[56] With its roots in material existence, this vision can grow and spread, opening up the possibility of becoming more fully human.

From a Canadian point of view, a sustainable world would have many elements we are already familiar with. The civil commons has been in action in this country in both the formal and informal sense: in the formal sense we see it in our version of the welfare state – universal health care, public education, and old-age security; in the informal sense we see it in meals on wheels, building bees, and community environmental clean-ups. What would be different would be the place of the civil commons in society.[57] It would not be an afterthought, or a concession, or something acknowledged only after some ever-elusive economic prosperity was achieved, or an evil to be stamped out as a manifestation of 'communism.' On the contrary, the civil commons would have pride of place in a sustainable world. It would be the axis around which all decisions rotated, the bottom line that could not be crossed, the raison d'être for policy and governance. Both formally and informally, we would live its options every minute of the day, orienting ourselves to its inclusive, universal entitlements, not to the exclusive, elite privileges of the global market.

As a cooperative human construct that protects and/or enables universal access to life goods, the civil commons can be built at many levels: local, provincial, federal, or global. Examples of each abound, from local bylaws on water quality to provincial education acts to federal health care legislation to global treaties on the environment. Multi-scalar, the civil commons provides crescent spaces where individual and community well-being can flourish, and the utopian project can be realized.

Many structures can advance the civil commons, such as governments, school boards, universities, community groups, and hospitals. This does not mean that they automatically build the civil commons, but that they have the potential. This potential is unleashed by the three building blocks of sustainability: counter-hegemony, dialogue, and life values. Built on this foundation, these structures can contribute to the civil commons.

Many processes can also advance the civil commons, such as teaching, learning, and researching. Once again, this does not mean that they automatically build the civil commons, but that they have the potential. This potential is also unleashed by the three building blocks of sustainability: counter-hegemony, dialogue, and life values. Built on this foundation, these processes can contribute to the civil commons.

Two examples will help to explain the alternative vision of sustainability envisioned in this book: education and health care.

Education
Education, in all its forms, has a long history of serving competing interests. As McMurtry states: 'Education has always been subject to external pressures that seek to subordinate its practice and goals to vested interests of some kind, whether of slave-holding oligarchies, theocratic states, political parties or merely prevailing dogmas of collective belief. The history of the development of social intelligence is largely a history of this conflict between the claims of education and inquiry, on the one hand, and the demands of ruling interests and ideologies on the other.'[57]

The dominant ruling interests today are transnational corporations. Their insatiable demands for ever-increasing returns to corporate stockholders and top-level management affects education on many levels. In the age of globalization, transnational corporations see education not as a public good or a basic human right, but as a privately owned, priced service to sell for a profit in the global market. They also see government regulation and the provision of public services such as education as barriers to trade in services.[58] For this reason, education is on the cusp of being converted to a service that only private producers can provide for a price.

In spite of the long history and current threats from dominant ruling interests, education also has a close association with the civil commons.

As an example of the civil commons in action, the entire practice of formal education can be decoded as the process of judging and enabling more comprehensive levels of thinking across defined breadths and depths of cognition.[59] Universal access to the life good of education has grown around the world with the increase in publicly funded education programs. In this way, public education has become a vital part of the civil commons, and the structures and processes that build it contribute to sustainability. Thus it is also linked to increased well-being and the realization of the utopian project. As the Caledon Institute for Social Policy affirms, 'high-quality public education advances the well-being of all citizens and helps us to accomplish some of our most cherished public purposes.'[60]

In the alternative vision of a sustainable world, education would be free of charge and publicly funded, from kindergarten through postdoctoral studies and continuing education – the result of the cooperative human construct of the civil commons that protects and/or enables universal access to the life good of education. Considering that both Ireland and Scotland recently abolished university tuition fees, this aspect of a sustainable world is readily achievable, providing the priority is education that enables more comprehensive levels of thinking, not profit extraction or training opportunities for transnational corporations. Those who preferred a private form of education would be free to do so, but at their own expense, not public expense. Schools would be kept open in rural communities not because they met some narrowly defined economic criteria of 'efficiency,' but because they contributed to a broader and deeper understanding of efficiency in terms of individual and community well-being on many levels. It is important to remember that schools also play a significant role in rural communities in terms of functions other than educational. They often house local cultural and political events, and serve as a physical resource for other activities.[61] Given this significance, local schools would be recognized not only as sources of resistance, but also as places where alternative visions could be created – vibrant centres of sustainability within rural communities.

The structures involved in this vision would include these local schools, as well as school boards, parent associations, ministries of education, neighbourhood groups, universities, and community colleges, to name a few. Built on the three building blocks of counter-hegemony, dialogue, and life values, these structures would contribute to the civil commons through every policy, decision, and choice they made. That contribution would be enabled by a number of processes, also built on the three building blocks. These processes would include teaching, learning, collaborating, and researching. In this way, by being an acknowledged part of the civil commons, education would contribute to sustainability and lead through the portal of well-being to the realization of being more fully human. The civil commons would be part of the curriculum at all levels – recognized, valorized, and prioritized.

Health Care

The twentieth century heralded the arrival of publicly funded health care in a number of countries around the world. In Canada, universal public health care came into being in the 1960s, spearheaded by Tommy Douglas in Saskatchewan and brought into law federally by the Conservative government of the day. In contrast to countries such as Canada, the United States developed a private health care system. Under this private system, the richest country in the world has health care which is $1,000 per capita more expensive than the Canadian system, fails to provide any health care to 48 million Americans, grossly underinsures another 30 million, and costs twice as much as the Canadian system in administrative bureaucracy.[62]

In the age of globalization, corporate health care is replacing more efficient and universally accessible public systems.[63] Seen as an enormous source of potential profits, public health care is under threat from transnational corporations, through the dictates of the World Trade Organization. Under the General Agreement on Trade in Services (GATS), health care, like education, is considered a service, and public funding of health-care systems is seen as a barrier to trade, and targeted for elimination.[64]

In the alternative vision of a sustainable world, health care would be universally accessible to all people – free of charge and publicly funded. This vision is borne out by McMurtry when he proposes that public health care for all people of a society without barriers of social caste or market cost is a major institution of a developed civil commons.[65]

The four pillars of the Canadian health care system are a shining model of the civil commons for the rest of the world: universality, accessibility, portability, and public administration. To prevent this example of the civil commons from being hijacked as a site of profit maximization for pharmaceutical companies, health management organizations, or private, for-profit practitioners, all health care would involve a single-tiered, well-funded, totally public system – the result of the cooperative human construct of the civil commons that protects and/or enables universal access to the life good of health care. Hospitals would be kept open in rural communities not because they met the narrow economic criteria of 'efficiency,' but because they contribute to the greater efficiency of individual and community well-being.[66] Decisions regarding the allocation of health care services would include those directly affected by these decisions, balancing local needs with state requirements. Rural areas would become creative sites of holistic community health care, not only responding to local circumstances, but also acting as stepping stones to more advanced levels of treatment. Publicly funded transportation would link people to hubs of centralized services.

The structures involved in this vision would include hospitals, ministries of health, boards of health, citizen forums, and community health clinics, to name a few. Built on the three building blocks of counter-hegemony, dialogue, and life values, these structures would contribute to the civil commons through every policy, decision, and choice they made. That contribution would be enabled by a number of processes, also built on the three building blocks, such as healing, researching, learning, advising, and counselling.

This chapter has put another vision of sustainability on the table, one that Canadians are familiar with but often do not recognize. Based on the optimum area of the theoretical model, a new understanding of sustainability involves a set of structures and processes that build the civil commons. Given our own history of engagement with the civil commons, the search for sustainability would not be very difficult for Canadians. What would be difficult would be moving it to the centre of our way of life.

6 New Directions for Research

Sustainability ... is politically treacherous since it challenges the status quo.[1]

A new understanding of sustainability that involves a set of structures and processes that build the civil commons provides a firm foundation for looking at some familiar terms from a fresh perspective. Giving new meaning to the mother concept of sustainability opens up the opportunity to look at some of the offspring of this fundamental idea and see what they could become in the age of globalization. This chapter will examine two familiar compound terms, *sustainable development* and *sustainable rural community*, and explore what they could mean when considered in light of a new understanding of sustainability. It will also put forward a new compound term, *sustainable globalization*, as a solution to the unrelenting destruction of corporate globalization.

Compound terms such as sustainable development and sustainable rural community are found throughout the academic literature, from economics to sociology to rural studies. Like sustainability itself, they are used in many different ways by many different people, resulting in conceptual confusion. To add to this confusion, these terms have even been used as justifications for patently unsustainable activities, such as structural adjustment programs.

Shearman argues that when we use sustainability as a modifier in compound terms such as sustainable development, it changes the way we come to understand the second half of those terms. In this way, 'sustainable' is used not only in a grammatical sense, as an adjective to a noun, but also in a conceptual sense, 'through the implication of a contradiction.' For Shearman, it implies that the status quo is inconsistent with the facts, and that the ends and means of current conceptions are incompatible. If not, then terms like sustainable development would be redundant.[2]

To take Shearman's argument one step further, working from a new understanding of sustainability as involving a set of structures and processes that build the civil commons means that in compound terms, the adjective 'sustainable' not only implies a contradiction, but also indicates a way out of the problem. Using the same building blocks that undergird a new understanding of sustainability, fresh insights can emerge from these familiar terms.

The compound terms, sustainable development and sustainable rural community, will serve to illustrate how such terms can change their meaning with a new understanding of sustainability.

A New Understanding of Sustainable Development

Like sustainability itself, sustainable development has become a widespread, popular term. While often used interchangeably, the two terms should be considered separately. Within the academic literature there are at least eighty different definitions of sustainable development or some part of it.[3] Many of these definitions, however, express the money code of value and explicitly promote corporate globalization.

Based on a new understanding of sustainability, *sustainable development involves development that is based on a set of structures and processes that build the civil commons.* These structures and processes must rest on the three building blocks of dialogue, counter-hegemony, and life values in order for them to be oriented towards constructing and protecting the civil commons.

Daly contributes to a new understanding of sustainable development when he uses dictionary definitions to differentiate between growth and development: '*To grow* means "to increase naturally in size by the addition of material through assimilation and accretion." *To develop* means "to expand or realize the potentialities of; bring gradually to a fuller, greater, or better state." In short, growth is quantitative increase in physical scale, while development is qualitative improvement or unfolding of potentialities.'[4]

A new understanding of sustainability allows for the unfolding of the potentialities of more than just the lucky few. Constructing and protecting the civil commons enables a *qualitative* improvement in the well-being of all individuals and communities, allowing them to develop in life-affirming ways. As McMurtry points out, 'no society ever develops by having starvation-wages for its people, loss of public revenues for its collective life security, and increasingly stripped natural resources.'[5]

The global growth machine, on the other hand, enables a *quantitative* increase in the assets of an ever-decreasing number of people, while the pernicious effects of such growth trickle down to the majority: environmental pollution, the increasing gap between rich and poor, and social fragmentation. The rhetoric of sustainable development has been used to veil its purpose of increasing market share, at any cost – even the lives of the poor. A good example of such rhetoric comes from the United Nations Development Program. In 1998, it launched an initiative to assist the two billion poorest people in the world called the Global Sustainable Development Facility – 2B2M: 2 Billion People to the Market by 2020. The aim was to establish an agency outside the UNDP, but closely related to it, through which those transnational corporations prepared to contribute a fee of $50,000 would have access to and benefit from association with the UNDP.[6] In this way, the money values of corporate globalization infiltrate and steer initiatives to help the world's poor – the elite set up the problems in their own terms and solve them to their own advantage. This strategy can be seen in conventional approaches to community economic development. Such approaches, according to Mark Roseland, often produce enormous amounts of pollution, consume huge quantities of energy and materials, fail to deliver sufficient jobs, promote underunemployment, result in disparity in distribution of economic benefits, or lead to corporate downsizing. For this reason, '"development" can no longer simply mean economic "growth," but requires instead that we learn to live on the "interest" generated by remaining stocks of "natural capital,"' and that we 'shift our economic development emphasis from the traditional concern with increasing growth to the new focus on reducing social dependence on economic growth.'[7]

Development that was truly sustainable would promote the civil commons, not the growth of the global market, as the key to development – protecting and enabling universal access to life goods instead of privatizing and profiting from them. With basic access to life goods assured, people could then improve their potential in ways not possible under conventional understandings of sustainable development.

How do other definitions of sustainable development in the academic literature measure up to this new understanding?

The most famous definition of sustainable development, without doubt, is the one contained in the Brundtland Report. According to this report, sustainable development is 'development that meets the needs of the present without compromising the ability of future generations to meet their own needs.'[8] Though ripe with possibilities, this definition promises much while delivering little. It is not based in any of the three building blocks of sustainability – counter-hegemony, dialogue, and life values – and does not mention any of the structures and processes that are involved in realizing sustainable development. Its very vagueness, backed up by a call for economic growth in the order of a five- to tenfold increase, accounts for the reason that 'corporations loved it because it validated their role as agents of progress.'[9] Furthermore, in the Brundtland Report, the bias is not just towards economic growth, but also towards international business as usual. Gains for the poor are conditioned on the maintenance and reform of the system that disadvantages them.[10]

A number of authors recognize certain aspects of a new understanding of sustainable development. Buttel acknowledges the lack of dialogue in some conceptualizations of sustainable development when he contends that sustainable development has strong managerialist overtones (of being top-down, bureaucratic, and disconnected from the concerns and preferences of the vast majority of people in the South). Barkin implies dialogue when he proposes that sustainable development is an approach to productive reorganization that encompasses the combined experiences of local groups throughout the world.[11] These authors, however, do not include an understanding of the aspects of counter-hegemony and life values, nor a recognition of the importance of structures and processes.

Fuller, Ehrensaft, and Gertler imply the possibility of a counter-hegemonic dimension for sustainable development, and an understanding of the importance of structures and processes, when they argue that it means 'satisfying present and future needs for material wellbeing while meeting co-objectives such as ecological stability. It also implies a rethinking of institutions and an exploration of new cultural terrain.'[12] However, this definition lacks a dialogue and a life-values dimension, and thus is not adequate to a new understanding of sustainable development.

Daly incorporates a counter-hegemonic dimension when he follows up his differentiation between growth and development with a description of sustainable development as 'a cultural adaptation made by society as it becomes aware of the emerging necessity of non-growth.'[13]

While this description incorporates a counter-hegemonic dimension by doing away with the growth emphasis exemplified by the Brundtland Report's definition of sustainable development, it offers little in the way of the dialogue or life values. The adaptation he proposes could still conceivably involve a top-down, money-centred vision of the world, with little place for the civil commons.

Some authors recognize the importance of life values for sustainable development. For example, Ruby Dunstan, Chief Emeritus of the Lytton First Nation, maintains that business as usual will not and cannot ensure global survival – sustainable development is about life, not about economics. Kumar, Manning, and Murck include life values and the counter-hegemonic undertones of carrying capacity when they see sustainable development as (1) Improving the quality of human life while living within the carrying capacity of supporting ecosystems; (2) meeting the needs of the present without compromising the ability of future generations to meet their own needs.[14] These definitions, however, do not include a dialogical aspect, nor do they recognize the importance of the structures and processes involved.

Some authors examine sustainable development specifically in terms of rurality. Day explains that 'Sustainable rural development is said to require patience, and the ability to take a long-term view; it takes time to bring about the active involvement of communities, to encourage the growth of local capacities, and to enlarge the scope of local leadership and self-determination.'[15]

This understanding emphasizes the importance of sustainable development to human agency and implies dialogue through active involvement, but involves neither counter-hegemony nor life values. Without those two building blocks, such development could end up supporting corporate globalization by encouraging the growth of local capacities to adapt to the global market and to enlarge the ability of local leadership to make this happen. It implies structures and processes, but does not highlight their importance.

Jones and Tonts use Redclift's definition of sustainable development in the rural context: 'sustainable rural development, however, requires a holistic and integrated approach which is concerned with "meeting human needs, or maintaining economic growth, or conserving natural capital, or about all three."'[16] Split into the subdivisions of economic, social, and environmental sustainability, this definition adds little to a concrete understanding of sustainable development. It does not include any of the building blocks, nor does it emphasize structures and processes.

All in all, these definitions lack a firm foundation on which to build the structures and processes involved in sustainable development. Without all three building blocks of dialogue, counter-hegemony, and life values, they fall short of providing a new understanding of sustainable development.

A New Understanding of Sustainable Rural Community

While rural community admits of many meanings, the one used throughout this book has been based on Paul Cloke's definition: a collection of socially interacting people living in a rural area, and often sharing one or more common ties.[17] These common ties are the basis of, and in turn can contribute to, the civil commons. Adding the word *sustainable* to the term *rural community* results in a compound concept with two implications: first, there is a contradiction and many rural communities are not, in fact, sustainable; second, there is a way out of this problem, and the solution is the civil commons. Based on the new understanding of sustainability, *a sustainable rural community involves a rural community that is based on a set of structures and processes that build the civil commons.* In rural communities, these structures and processes would be multi-scalar; that is, they could be global, national, provincial, or local in nature. Although communities would be the beneficiaries of the civil commons built at the international, national, or provincial level (such as education and health care), they would also include their own structures and processes that contribute to it at the local level in order to reflect in particular the differences among rural communities. For example, coastal communities would be involved not only in a multi-scalar web of structures and processes that build cooperative human constructs to ensure universal access to life goods in general, but also to life goods dealing with fishing in particular.

The structures and processes need not be different across the country in order to reflect the diversity of Canadian rural communities. For instance, the Women's Institute in a remote community could work towards improved medical services, while the Women's Institute in the rural-urban fringe could campaign for bylaws to prohibit big box stores like Wal-Mart. The same structure contributes to the civil commons, but in different ways in different locations.

A new understanding of sustainability means that sustainability in rural communities would revolve around constructing and protecting the civil commons, not around economic growth. Using the growth-machine hypothesis, Bridger and Harp explain how, under many circumstances, local growth constitutes a transfer of quality-of-life and wealth from the local general public to a certain segment of the local elite.[18]

In a telling article on poverty and social context in remote rural communities, Duncan and Lamborghini compare a chronically poor coal-dependent Appalachian rural community with a more diverse, resource-rich rural community in northern New England. They found that the overwhelming pattern in the Appalachian community was one of social isolation – the poor led one kind of life and the non-poor another. Generosity and outreach, trust and cooperation, were the exception rather than the rule. In contrast, in the New England community, there appeared to be widespread participation in community affairs and regular exchange between people with widely differing occupations and income levels. Neither the poor nor the non-poor were isolated. One of the main differences between these two rural communities is the existence in the New England community of a wide range of public goods that are available to everyone. Under such circumstances, 'poor people benefit because they are not stigmatized and socially separated from affluent families and because the public sector on which they depend so greatly is also used by the middle class and is of better quality. They have more real opportunity to work, find social support, and get a good education, and their experiences appear to have given them more confidence that they can take advantage of opportunities and move out of poverty.'[19]

In other words, a strong civil commons protects and enables universal access to life goods in rural communities. This access provides opportunities that would not otherwise exist for many people, such as education, income support, social inclusion, job opportunities, and networking. When the civil commons is strong, people thrive, and the result can be improved individual and community well-being.

When the civil commons is attacked and weakened (as exemplified by the growth-machine hypothesis), many people are left behind, excluded from the benefits enjoyed by those who can afford to pay for them. Exclusion and fragmentation were evident in the Appalachian community. The authors cite Coleman when they suggest that 'the whole social fabric weakens because investment in public goods and collective well-being is minimal.'[20]

This research highlights the importance of a new understanding of sustainability that includes the civil commons. Such an understanding embraces everyone, inviting them to participate, to question, and to affirm what they already unconsciously know – that life in all its wildly divergent forms does not exist to serve money, but that money exists to serve life.

How do other definitions of sustainable rural community in the academic literature measure up to a new understanding of sustainable rural community as a rural community that involves a set of structures and processes that build the civil commons?

Fuller, Ehrensaft, and Gertler contend that sustainable rural communities must be forward-looking communities, places where women and men of all backgrounds will choose to make a life, as well as be able to make a living.[21] This description has none of the building blocks of a new understanding of sustainability: it does not include dialogue, counter-hegemony or life values (although the idea of choice could be construed as a precursor to life values). In addition, there is no mention of the structures and processes that contribute to sustainability. In this way, it cannot help us in our search for a new understanding of sustainable rural communities.

Some authors define sustainable rural communities in terms of a number of subdivisions of sustainability. For example, in the Guelph Seminar Series on sustainable rural communities, Bryden suggests that a sustainable community is one which exhibits certain features of economic, social, cultural, and ecological sustainability. Similarly, in their article in the *Journal of Rural Studies* concerning an interactional approach to community development, Bridger and Luloff define sustainable communities as ones that meet the economic needs of their residents, enhance and protect the environment, and promote more humane local societies. In the same vein, Hart maintains that a sustainable community seeks to maintain and improve the economic, environmental, and social characteristics of an area so its members can continue to lead healthy, productive, enjoyable lives there.[22] These descriptions have none of the building blocks of a new understanding of sustainability, nor any recognition of the structures and processes that contribute to the civil commons. For these reasons, they are also not adequate to a new understanding of sustainable rural communities in the age of globalization.

Berry addresses our relationship to the natural environment when he describes a sustainable community as 'a neighbourhood of humans in a place, plus the place itself: its soil, its water, its air, and all the families and tribes of nonhuman creatures that belong to it ... we are speaking of a complex connection not only among human beings and homeland but also between the human economy and nature, between forest and field or orchard, and between troublesome creatures and pleasant ones. *All neighbours are included.*'[23]

While this description has none of the building blocks of sustainability, and none of the structures and processes associated with sustainability, it does open up the notion of inclusion that is inherent in the civil commons.

Scott, Park, and Cocklin want to do away with the concept of sustainable rural community altogether, relegating it to a 'folk category, not as part of our social science discourse.' They propose resorting to the broader concept of social sustainability, which for them has 'a local, historically defined content which will include elements of livelihood, social participation, justice and equity.'[24] Such a move would eliminate the possibility of a more general understanding of sustainability, which would bind people from different communities together. The universal aspects of the civil commons call for an understanding of sustainable rural communities that includes, but is also more than, local considerations.

Sustainable Globalization

While at first appearing to be some absurd oxymoron, the term *sustainable globalization* exemplifies Shearman's contention that modifying a noun with the adjective 'sustainable' implies a contradiction – that the status quo is inconsistent with the facts. Nowhere does this seem more evident than in the term sustainable globalization. Environmental despoliation, the widening gap between rich and poor, and the monumental power of transnational corporations all seem to make a cruel mockery of the hope that globalization could be sustainable.

And yet, as discussed in Chapter 1, there is more than one kind of globalization. The globalization from below instantiated by social movements works to counter the globalization from above promoted by corporate globalization. Although the term sustainable globalization has the potential to be co-opted by those who support corporate globalization, it is better to stake the territory early, applying a contestable term to individual and community well-being, than to try to wrestle it away at a later date from those who would use it to prosper from corporate globalization.

A term such as sustainable globalization could also help to prevent corporate globalization from eventually becoming the only kind of glo-

balization we live under. Sustainable globalization could become a rally-
ing point for resistance and alternative visions, pointing out, by its very
existence, the dead end of corporate globalization.

Just adding sustainable globalization to the current lexicon could also
change the way people understand globalization. Like the Trojan Horse,
it could introduce a small but potent opposition into the seemingly
impenetrable territory of corporate globalization. Beveridge argues that
a major weakness in the globalization agenda is its neglect of sustainability
issues.[25] It is time to expose that weakness through a term like sustainable globalization, and occupy the higher ground of the civil commons.

Adding sustainable globalization to our everyday understanding of
the world could provide a vibrant alternative to the TINA (there is no
alternative) syndrome of corporate globalization. The human agency
inherent in a new understanding of sustainability would allow sustainable globalization to highlight the lie of the so-called inevitability of
corporate globalization that can paralyse opposition to it.

If sustainability involves a set of structures and processes that build the
civil commons, then *sustainable globalization would be understood as globalization that is based on a set of structures and processes that build the civil
commons.* Some of these structures could include the United Nations,
the International Council for Adult Education, Amnesty International,
Doctors Without Borders, Greenpeace, and the Sierra Legal Defence
Fund. Some of these processes would be the same as those involved
in sustainability itself: learning, teaching, facilitating, researching, collaborating, and decision-making.

As a global phenomenon, these structures and processes would work
for the civil commons at the supranational level. This is not an impossible task. We have already been working for the civil commons beyond
the borders of the nation state. Current examples of such work include
the Amsterdam Treaty on dumping, the Kyoto agreement on climate
change, the European Union (in its aspects that protect or enable
universal access to life goods, such as minimum wages and free movement of labour), the United Nations Convention on the Rights of the
Child, and the United Nations Universal Declaration of Human Rights.
Future examples could include investment and speculation taxes, international workers' rights legislation, and anti-racism treaties, to name a
few.

In answer to those who would argue that sustainable globalization
could never work, it is important to point out that corporate globalization works, so why not sustainable globalization? The regulation of

governments and communities around the world through the imposition of transnational trade agreements belies any statement that it cannot be done.

But how has this regulation been achieved? Far from inevitable or
God-given, corporate globalization is built through decisions made every
day in corporate boardrooms, government departments, municipal meetings, and university administration offices. In his article on social movements for global capitalism, Sklair argues that global capitalism has to
struggle to create and reproduce its hegemonic order globally: 'The
capitalist class expends much time, energy and resources to make it
happen, and to ensure that it keeps on happening.' One of the ways in
which the transnationalist capitalist class achieves its aims, Sklair contends, is through social movements. These elite social movement organizations (ESMOs) are different from the non-elite social movements such
as environmental, labour, peace, and human rights movements that we
generally associate with globalization from below: 'The high social status
of ESMO members makes it likely that these organizations will rely on
finance and expertise rather than personnel and mass-based activities.'[26]

This argument is reminiscent of George's discussion of how the Right
has bought and paid for its ascendancy, in particular tracing the rise of
Francis Fukuyama as one of the spokespeople specially selected and
groomed to promote the corporate agenda.[27] Both authors argue, in
effect, that corporate globalization is achieved step by step, advancing
through decisions made at every level every day. For just as sustainability
involves a set of structures and processes that build the civil commons
(the common-wealth), corporate globalization involves a set of structures and processes that build the private wealth of a very few people.
The International Monetary Fund,[28] the World Bank, the Trilateral
Commission, the Fraser Institute, the World Trade Organization, and
the Canadian Council of Chief Executives are some of the structures
that build corporate globalization. Many of the processes – such as
decision-making, teaching, learning, and writing – are the same processes that are also part of sustainability. It depends what they build:
private wealth for the few, or the civil commons.

Those who promote sustainable globalization would generally not
have the money to buy their way onto the world agenda, like those who
promote corporate globalization. As Sklair explained, they rely on personnel and mass-based activities. The demonstrations that accompany
meetings of the WTO or the G7 are just one example of such mass-based
activities. These activities have an effect on the forces of corporate

globalization, prompting them to begin to justify their activities in more than purely economic terms. Held argues that the twentieth century has seen the beginning of significant efforts to reframe markets – to use legislation to alter the background conditions and operations of firms in the marketplace. While he contends that these efforts failed with respect to NAFTA, they succeeded with the 'Social Chapter' of the Maastricht Treaty, setting down 'new forms of regulation which can be built upon.' For Held, these examples of changes in global politics and regulations suggest that 'while globalization is a highly contested phenomenon, it has embraced important collaborative initiatives in politics, law and the economy in the 20th century. Together, these create an anchor on which to build a more accountable form of globalization.'[29]

Sustainable globalization can be a more accountable form of globalization because it involves structures and processes that build the civil commons. In this way, it is accountable to life interests, not the distorted, life-appropriating demands of money interests. Its collaborative initiatives create an anchor on which to build an alternative vision to corporate globalization, one that can realize the dreams of more than a small minority of people. In this way, sustainable globalization can become an alternative utopian vision to the dystopia of corporate globalization, and could even be labelled what Prugh, Costanza, and Daly refer to as genotopia: the place that is continually unfolding, being born, and reborn.[30]

Living in the Age of Sustainable Globalization

Rural communities in Canada face increasing challenges to their sustainability. The economic, political, social, environmental, gender-based, and cultural impacts of corporate globalization deeply affect their choices, now and into the future. The crisis of sustainability is nowhere clearer than in rural communities, which are 'struggling to provide the quality of life and livelihood for which many Canadians secretly yearn.'[31]

An alternative to the destructive impacts of corporate globalization is one that is already available to us, but beneath consciousness – the civil commons, which is 'the middle term between life and more comprehensive life.'[32] We can build on this common heritage, making a new understanding of sustainability part of our conscious, everyday lives, and building up the structures and processes that support the civil commons, instead of watching them get broken down by the forces of corporate globalization. The policies that promote this breakdown are designed to eliminate the civil commons while ensuring that no place can escape being a source or a sink for profit maximization.

In the stitch-by-stitch effort to make us believe in the benefits of corporate globalization, those who promote it have encouraged the rest of us to turn our backs on the civil commons and imagine that our future well-being lies with the global market. But the global market is simply incapable of protecting and enabling universal access to life goods, which is why the civil commons is so important to the well-being of individuals and communities. Gordon Laxer reminds us that 'the global market is the arena for transnationals, business professionals and the rich, where power is based on unequal command of property.'[33] There is no room in this arena for the civil commons, and the universal benefits that it can bring to rural communities.

A new understanding of sustainability can start within rural communities themselves, evolving through local initiatives towards the wider world. Working from the heritage of the already-existing civil commons, community members can use structures and engage in processes that build the civil commons locally as well as nationally and globally.

Part of working together involves resistance. In contrast to the deterministic belief that resistance is futile, graffiti on a wall in downtown Guelph, Ontario, proclaims that resistance is *fertile*. There is no doubt that there is a great deal of local, networked resistance to corporate globalization. Sklair emphasizes the importance of resistance at the local level when he reminds us that 'the resistances to global capitalism can only be effective where they can disrupt its smooth running (accumulation of private profits) locally and can find ways of globalizing these disruptions.'[34]

One way to globalize disruptions is to share local initiatives with other communities, which not only has disruptive power, but also allows communities to network and learn from each other, acting as agents in their own sustainability. Some communities have already acted locally to stand up against corporate globalization, including outlawing corporate non-family ownership of farmland and proposing a 'ten strikes and you're out' ordinance for corporations with more than ten pollution infractions.[35]

But resistance is not the only option for local communities. The alternative visions that must accompany resistance need to look ahead to something better. The Zapatistas of Mexico provide an example of this alternative visioning:

What we are talking about now is localization as a word that is both opposite to globalization and localism ... There is a sense that what we had before Zapatismo was a form of localism in which people were resisting in their small communities and concentrating their forces internally ... What we are now describing is a transition from resistance to liberation, because people are still rooted in their own place, committed to that place, strengthening their roots in that place, but also opening themselves to wide coalitions of others like them, looking for solidarity, mutual support, new ideas, learning from others.[36]

From Local Communities to the Nation State

Nation states stand between local communities and global powerhouses – the transnational corporations. The policies of corporate globalization include a changing role for government: moving from regulating corporations to creating conditions conducive to corporate activity. In age of globalization, the role of the nation state involves promoting a favourable investment climate for transnational corporations.

For this and other reasons, many individuals and communities look beyond the nation state to the global situation. However, thinking globally but acting locally undermines the state as an arena of collective action.[37] In spite of its shortcomings and outright pandering to transnational corporations, the nation state is crucial to a new understanding of sustainability. The nation state is currently the best vehicle we have for the universalization of the formal aspects of the civil commons. Few other entities are capable of guaranteeing universal access to life goods such as health care and education.[38] If we did away with the nation state, who, for example, would guarantee and enforce our constitutional rights under the Charter of Rights and Freedoms? The community is not powerful enough, and any global mechanism is completely lacking.

In the face of growing inequalities produced by corporate globalization, nation states are no longer even able to legislate social policies that could promote the well-being of their own citizens. But this incapacity has not always existed nor does it have to be the case in the future. The changing role of the state, from regulator of the public good to being regulated by transnational trade agreements, can be reversed.

In an ideal world, the civil commons and the nation state would merge. In the real world, we can work towards this goal by strengthening the ability of the nation state to provide the means of life for more than just the elite. Transnational corporations have a place in a world oriented to sustainable globalization, but a well-regulated place, which would curtail their ability to supersede life needs by corporate demands.

From the National to the International

When discussing sustainability, Buttel asserts that while conceptions of the dynamics of states and capital can be helpful in understanding the constraints on sustainability in the North, they are not readily generalizable to the South. In spite of this assertion, a new understanding of sustainability with Canadian roots has a role to play in global sustainability. 'The gift that Canada can offer to the world is a globalization that is the narrative of sharing for survival.'[39] Sharing for survival is at the heart of sustainability because it is at the heart of the civil commons. Protecting and enabling universal access to life goods, in order to reproduce or enhance the ranges of life of everyone, is the mark of a civilized world. Canada has led the way in instantiating this advancement. Corporate globalization, which increasingly restricts access to life goods to only an elite group who can afford to ante up in the global casino, is the mark of regressive barbarism.

Marsden recognizes the effects of this restriction in rural communities when he contends that 'we can start to see in rural areas the development of a much more diverse set of privatized consumption relations *at the same time* as we witness ... the state-supported diminution of the remaining vestiges of collective consumption and welfare.'[40]

In a world dominated by corporate globalization, if you cannot become a private consumer, you have no right to live. As the collective good is replaced by corporate demand, the power of the collective is lost in the fragmentation of individual desires, leaving those unable to look after themselves in the brave new world of corporate globalization blamed for their own problems and left alone to solve them. This loss of collective orientation is clearly evident in rural communities under stress: 'Communities unable to act collectively to ensure survival are those destined to decline ... Such communities may have people living within the recognizable boundaries, but their orientation is neither local nor cooperative. It is not population change per se that dooms a community but failing collectively to rebuild or revitalize it.'[41]

The civil commons represents the collective will of communities of all kinds to assure universal access to life goods for all members. Whether at the local, national, or international level, the civil commons is the collective key to sustainability, increased individual and community well-being, and the realization of the utopian vision.

In the final analysis, sustainability raises questions about the nature of the good society. Is the good society one in which fewer and fewer people own more and more wealth, draining the communal resources of individuals, communities and the natural environment, or is the good society one in which more and more people share the common-wealth, preserving and enhancing it for future generations? The former is the path of corporate globalization; the latter is the path of sustainable globalization, if sustainability is based on the three building blocks of counter-hegemony, dialogue, and life values, and involves a set of structures and processes that build the civil commons.

As mentioned in the introduction to this volume, understanding sustainability is very similar to the problem of understanding life itself. It is more than similar – it is synonymous. Understanding sustainability means understanding what builds life and what destroys it. The civil commons is life centred, protecting or enabling universal access to life goods in order to provide the means of reproducing or enhancing life in all its vital ranges of thought, feeling, and action. Sustainability protects the civil commons and the civil commons protects means of life in a web of grounded choices that steward the natural environment, promote the well-being of individuals and communities, and open the way for the realization of being more fully human.

Notes

Introduction

1 Robinson et al. 'Defining a Sustainable Society,' 36.
2 Rees, 'Globalization and Sustainability,' 255; United Nations, *Least Developed Countries Report 2002: Escaping the Poverty Trap*, unctad.org/en/pub/ps1ldc02.en.htm; Sussman, *Communication, Technology and Politics*, 14.
3 'Rural,' 'community,' and 'rural community' are all complex and contested terms. Keeping in mind these complexities and arguments, and the extensive literature surrounding them, I follow Paul Cloke's definition of rural community: 'a collection of socially interacting people living in a rural area, and often sharing one or more common ties.' See Cloke, *Dictionary of Human Geography*, 718.
4 Solomon, 'Coast-to-Coast Subsidies,' C15.
5 McMurtry, *Unequal Freedoms*, 298.
6 *Encyclopaedia Britannica* online at http://www.britannica.com.
7 Bullock and Trombley, *Fontana Dictionary*, 889.
8 Hart, *Working and Educating*, 214.
9 Carr, 'Globalization from Below,' 49. Carr begins his article on globalization from below with the observation that 'globalization is frequently presented as an inexorable "steamroller" drive towards internationalization of politics and economics following a logic set by big investors and traders.'
10 Quoted in Gonick, 'A Democratic Socialist Vision,' 39.
11 One of the components of that dream is the so-called 'rural idyll,' defined by Jo Little and Patricia Austin as the positive images surrounding many aspects of the rural lifestyle, community, and landscape, reinforcing, at its simplest, healthy, peaceful, secure, and prosperous representations of

rurality. These images are not without problems, however, because embedded within them are questions about who created them and who benefits from them. But the concept of the rural idyll is not without merit. Joan Iverson Nassauer argues that the popular image of the countryside is a visual metaphor for human life in harmony with nature. For Nassauer, it is 'an intentional way to achieve popular support for serious ends: ecological health, agricultural production, and quality of life.' It is no accident that popular images of rural do not include monocultures, pesticide sprayers, suburban development, intensive livestock operations, or E-coli in the drinking water. Rather than dismissing the rural idyll as a false construction, we can use it to raise questions, promote change, and encourage a closer connection between image and reality. See Little and Austin, 'Women and the Rural Idyll,' 101; Nassauer, 'Agricultural Landscapes,' 57.

12 Simpson and Weiner, *Oxford English Dictionary*, 122.
13 Fromm, *The Art of Loving*.
14 Sachs, *Planet Dialectics*, 186.
15 Prugh, Costanza, and Daly, *Local Politics*, 44
16 Doob, *Sustainers and Sustainability*, 5.
17 Prugh, Costanza, and Daly, *Local Politics*, 17.
18 Peacock, 'Second Law of Thermodynamics,' 1.
19 Laxer, 'Radical Transformative Nationalisms,' 133.
20 Brecher, Costello, and Smith, *Globalization from Below*, 4.
21 United Nations Development Program (UNDP). *Human Development Report 2003*. New York: Oxford University Press, 2003.
22 Brecher, Costello, and Smith, *Globalization from Below*, ix.
23 Ibid., 17.
24 For example, Laxer, ('Radical Transformative Nationalisms,' 141) argues that much of the globalization-from-below rhetoric is anti-national, while some of it is opposed to national sovereignty as well. But the nation state is crucial to any vision of sustainability because, as yet, no global institutions can guarantee such life-sustaining measures as public health care or public education.
25 McMurtry, 'Life-Ground,' 822, 828, 834, 836, 837, 842.
26 Ibid., 822, 828.

Chapter 1. The Age of Globalization

1 Levis, 'Global Circus,' 3.
2 Godínez, 'Economía Mundial,' 25.
3 Simpson and Weiner, *Oxford English Dictionary*, 582.

4 Therborn, 'Introduction,' 149; Therborn, 'Globalizations,' 172.
5 Meyer, 'Globalization,' 233; Therborn, 'Globalizations,' 151–3.
6 Therborn, 'Globalizations,' 158–63; Shiva, 'Ecological Balance,' 48.
7 Mel Watkins, 'Canadian Capitalism in Transition,' in Wallace Clement (ed.), *Understanding Canada: Building on the New Canadian Political Economy* (Montreal and Kingston: McGill-Queen's University Press, 1977), 19; Careless, *Frontier and Metropolis*, 8–9.
8 Careless, *Frontier and Metropolis*, 9, 39.
9 Harold A. Innis, 'Economic Nationalism,' from papers and proceedings of the Canadian Political Science Association, 6 (1934): 17–31, in Drache, *Staples, Markets*, 218; Careless, *Frontier and Metropolis*, 96.
10 Watkins, 'Canadian Capitalism in Transition,' 33.
11 Wallerstein, 'Age of Transition,' 250. See also Immanuel Wallerstein, *The Essential Wallerstein* (New York: New Press, 2000), 207, 469.
12 David Harvey, *Spaces of Capital: Towards a Critical Geography* (New York: Routledge, 2001), 403; David Harvey, *The Condition of Postmodernity: An Enquiry into the Origins of Cultural Change* (Cambridge, Mass.: Blackwell, 1990), 129, 135, 140, 188.
13 Harvey, *Condition of Postmodernity*, 147, 156, 186.
14 Ibid., 123, 124.
15 Ibid., vii, 196.
16 Albrow, 'Globalization,' 248; Ratner, 'Many Davids, One Goliath,' 271.
17 McMurtry, *Value Wars*.
18 Mazur, 'Labor's New Internationalism,' 84.
19 Williams, 'Church Debates Market Economy,' B5; Lind, 'Rural Population of Saskatchewan.'
20 Barkin, 'Sustainability,' 20.
21 World Bank, 'Globalization, Growth and Poverty'; Dollar and Kraay, 'Spreading the Wealth'; Schmukler and Zoido-Lobatón, 'Financial Globalization'; *Economist*, 'Case for Globalization,' 19.
22 Brummer, 'Globalization'; Albrow, 'Globalization,' 249; Bhagwati, 'Coping with Antiglobalization,' 3.
23 Quoted in *CCPA Monitor*, 'Corporate Takeover,' 24.
24 Ibid., 25.
25 Ibid.
26 *Economist*, 'Case for Globalization,' 19.
27 The Globalism Project.
28 Skinner, 'Respond to Globalization?'
29 Ibid., 15; Dollar and Kraay, 'Spreading the Wealth,' 121, 127; Bhagwati, 'Coping with Antiglobalization,' 3.

30 Dollar and Kraay, 'Spreading the Wealth,' 131; Bhagwati, 'Coping with Antiglobalization,' 6.

31 Dollar and Kraay, 'Spreading the Wealth,' 120; *Economist*, 'Case for Globalization,' 19; World Bank.

32 *Economist*, 'Case for Globalization,' 19.

33 Skinner, 'Respond to Globalization,' 15.

34 *Economist*, 'Case for Globalization,' 19, 85.

35 In Bygrave, 'All the Protesters,' 21.

36 Soros, 'Capitalist Threat,' 52.

37 Palast, 'Globalizer.'

38 This life-blind economic program has been referred to by John Ralston Saul as 'the crucifixion theory of economics: you had to be killed economically and socially in order to be reborn clean and healthy.' See Saul. 'Collapse of Globalism,' 38.

39 Daly, 'Globalization versus Internationalization,' 34.

40 McMurtry, *Cancer Stage of Capitalism*, 38–41. See especially his table (p. 40) outlining the differences between the real free market and the corporate system.

41 Lind, 'Rural Population of Saskatchewan,' 6; Kerr, 'Women's Rights,' 9.

42 Ellwood describes how the theory of comparative advantage was developed in 1817 by British economist David Ricardo. Ricardo believed that nations should specialize in producing goods in which they have a natural advantage and thereby find their market niche. This belief was predicated on certain conditions, such as balanced trade between partners and the prevention of capital flows. See Ellwood, *No-Nonsense Guide*, 16.

43 Daly, 'Globalization versus Internationalization,' 32.

44 George, 'War of Ideas.'

45 Berry, 'Death of Rural Community,' 184.

46 Brittain and Elliott, 'World's Poor,' 23.

47 McMurtry, 'Caging the Poor,' 179.

48 Brecher, Childs, and Cutler, *Global Visions*, xv.

49 Falk, 'Making of Global Citizenship,' 39.

50 Brecher and Costello. *Global Village*, 106, 9.

51 Hunter, 'Globalization from Below?' 7.

52 Kingsnorth, 'Heads of the Hydra,' 203.

53 Marshall, 'Globalization from Below,' 67.

54 Gill, 'Reflections on Global Order,' 311.

55 Hall, 'Global Civil Society,' 11.

56 Ibid., 24.

57 Gramsci, *Prison Notebooks*, 12.

58 Mayo, *Gramsci, Freire*, 10.

Chapter 2. Rural Reckoning

1 Statement by Julio Terrazas, the archbishop of Santa Cruz and the president of the Episcopal Conference of Bolivia. Cited in Therborn, 'Globalizations,' 152.

2 Norberg-Hodge, 'Turning the Globalisation Tide,' 202.

3 J.M.S. Careless, *Frontier and Metropolis: Regions, Cities, and Identities in Canada before 1914* (Toronto: University of Toronto Press 1989), 9, 61.

4 Ibid., 12, 13.

5 Ibid., 35. See also Innis. 'Economic Nationalism,' 17–31.

6 Drache, *Staples, Markets, and Cultural Change*, xxii.

7 Norcliffe, 'Canadian Newsprint Industry,' 2–6.

8 Reed, 'Jobs Talk,' 755–63.

9 Flora, 'Presidential Address,' 157.

10 Harvey, *Spaces of Capital*, 402–3; Harvey, 'From Managerialism to Entrepreneurialism,' 3–17.

11 Harvey, 'From Managerialism to Entrepreneurialism,' 1, 15.

12 Mitchell, 'Entrepreneurialism,' 276, 283–4. The entrepreneurial mindset, based in money values, can be destructive to rural communities. Gregory Palast, a journalist living in small-town America, argues that for sheer narrow-minded, corrosive greed, nothing can beat the USA's grasping, whingeing small businessmen. And within that avaricious little pack, none are so poisonously self-centred and incorrigible as the small-town business-men of rural America. See Palast, 'Ugliness of Pleasantville USA.'

13 Barnes and Hayter, 'Little Town That Did,' 647–63.

14 Suzuki, 'Corporate Agriculture'; Qualman, 'Corporate Hog Farming,' 22; Ikerd, 'Destructive Factory Farms,' 1.

15 Kimbrell, 'Seven Deadly Myths,' 3; Padavic, 'Agricultural Restructuring,' 210.

16 Lind, 'Rural Population of Saskatchewan,' 6–7; Canadian Press, 'Rural Way of Life,' A13; Qualman, 'Fight for the Family Farm,' 3; Bailey, 'All the People Gone?' 22.

17 Wimberly, review of *Global Restructuring of Agro-Food Systems*, 538; National Farmers Union, 'People's Summit,' 18.

18 Lobao, 'Industrialized Farming,' 1.

19 Duncan, 'Understanding Persistent Poverty,' 108.

20 McMurtry, *Unequal Freedoms*, 249; McMurtry, *Cancer Stage of Capitalism*, 71; McMichael, 'Globalization: Myths and Realities,' 34, 35. The importance of debt can be understood by the fact that General Motors and General Electric, for example, 'both made more profits in 1994 from their financial subsidiaries lending credit-money at compound interest than they did from

all of their production of automotive and electrical manufactures put
together' (McMurtry, *Cancer Stage of Capitalism*, 121).

21 Flora, 'Presidential Address,' 163; Smailes, 'Socio-economic Change' 22;
Lorenz, et al., 'Rural Husbands and Wives,' 265.

22 Freudenburg, 'Addictive Economies,' 308; Ciccantell, 'Globalization,' 24.

23 Foley, 'Adult Education and Capitalist Reorganisation,' 122, 138–9;
McMichael, 'Globalization,' 38.

24 Jones and Tonts, 'Rural Restructuring,' 135, 137.

25 Flora and Flora, 'Entrepreneurial Social Infrastructure,' 55; Kristof, 'Life for
Family Farmers'; Swaim, 'Adapting to Economic Change,' 230; Duncan and
Lamborghini, 'Poverty and Social Context,' 443.

26 Norcliffe, 'Regional Labour Market Adjustments' 10.

27 Coates, 'Northland,' 113; Ciccantell, 'Globalization,' 22–4.

28 Lauzon and Hagglund, 'From the Ground Up,' 6; Kristoff, 'Life for Family
Farmers.'

29 Bell and Cloke, 'The Changing Relationship Between the Private and Public
Sectors: Privatisation and Rural Britain.' *Journal of Rural Studies*, vol. 5, no. 1
(1980): 4, 11.

30 McMichael, 'Globalization,' 46.

31 Wilson, 'Rural Restructuring,' 419–20, 430.

32 Sussman, *Communication, Technology and Politics*, 284. See also George, 'Short
History of Neo-liberalism,' 5–6. This privatizing agenda has been promoted
by unregulated supranational institutions such as the World Bank, which, by
1991, had made 114 loans to speed up the privatization process (George,
'Short History of Neo-liberalism,' 5).

33 Bell and Cloke, 'Private and Public Sectors,' 6, 8.

34 Ibid., 8, 14.

35 McMichael, 'Globalization,' 40.

36 Leach and Winson. 'Bringing Globalization Down to Earth,' 345;
McLaughlin, Gardner and Lichter, 'Economic Restructuring,' 394.

37 Marsden, 'Exploring a Rural Sociology,' 222.

38 Leach and Winson, 'Bringing Globalization Down to Earth,' 349; Marsden,
'Exploring a Rural Sociology,' 223.

39 Albrecht, 'Industrial Transformation,' 60–1.

40 Mitchell, 'Entrepreneurialism,' 283. The *rural idyll* is itself is a contested
term, and can serve as a form of repression. For example, Jo Little and
Patricia Austin argue that the rural idyll is instrumental in shaping and
sustaining patriarchal gender relations, and that it incorporates, both
consciously and unconsciously, strong expectations concerning aspects of
household strategy and gender roles, and consequently impacts on the

nature of women's experience within the rural community. See Little and Austin, 'Rural Idyll,' 102.

41 Coates, 'Northland,' 123.

42 Wilson, 'Agriculture-Rural Economy Linkages,' 419; Lobao, 'Industrialized Farming.'

43 McMurtry, *Cancer Stage of Capitalism*, 54.

44 Norcliffe, 'Regional Labour Market Adjustments,' 14.

45 Leach and Winson, 'Bringing Globalization Down to Earth,' 248, 349.

46 Swaim, 'Adapting to Economic Change,' 213.

47 Berry, 'Conserving Communities,' 408; Barnes and Hayter, 'Little Town That Did,' 654; Canadian Broadcasting Corporation, CBC Radio News (30 January 2000); Coates, 'Northland,' 111.

48 Thrift, 'Commodification,' 78.

49 Marsden, 'Restructuring Rurality,' 314–15.

50 Mitchell, 'Entrepreneurialism,' 273, 275.

51 Blanc, 'Family Farming,' 288.

52 Mitchell, 'Entrepreneurialism.'

53 Ward, et al., 'Rural Restructuring and the Regulation of Farm Pollution,' 1193; Marsden, 'Fordist Tradition,' 221.

54 Jones and Tonts, 'Rural Restructuring,' 138.

55 Jackson, 'Commodity Cultures,' 104; Thrift, 'Geography of Consumption,' 109.

56 Shiva, 'Economic Globalization,' 25.

57 Elliott, 'Blind Greed,' 14.

58 Silva, 'Politics of Sustainable Development,' 483.

59 Bell and Cloke, 'Private and Public Sectors,' 11.

60 Wilson, 'Agriculture–Rural Economy Linkages,' 419.

61 Smailes, 'Socio-economic Change,' 40; Jacob, Bourke, and Luloff, 'Rural Community Stress,' 275, 276; Bell and Cloke, 'Private and Public Sectors,' 10.

62 Rivera, 'Impacts of Extension Privatization.'

63 Pawson and Scott, 'Regional Consequences,' 384. The authors add that this promotion of enterprise is accompanied by an ideology of self-reliance, which stresses the virtues of small business and self-employment while leading a sustained assault on the welfare state.

64 Bell and Cloke, 'Private and Public Sectors,' 8.

65 Lauzon and Leahy, 'Educational Reform.'

66 Jacob, Bourke, and Luloff, 'Rural Community Stress,' 275; Lauzon and Hagglund, 'From the Ground Up,' 20.

67 Lorenz et al., 'Economic Conditions,' 248; Jacob, Bourke, and Luloff, 'Rural Community Stress,' 275, 276.

68 Ciccantell, 'Globalization,' 22–3. See also Jones and Tonts, 'Rural Restructuring,' 137.
69 Cloke, 'State Deregulation,' 46.
70 Blanc, *Family Farming*, 288.
71 Ward et al., 'Regulation of Farm Pollution,' 1194; Salamon and Tornatore, 'Territory Contested,' 638, 652.
72 Jones and Tonts, 'Rural Restructuring,' 134.
73 Goldsmith, 'Can the Environment Survive,' 242.
74 Berry, 'Conserving Communities,' 408.
75 Buttell, 'Some Observations,' 279; Barkin, 'Sustainability,' 23.
76 Khor, 'Development, Trade and the Environment,' 39.
77 Reed, 'Endangered Forests and Endangered Communities.' This quotation helps to illustrate the complexity of the relationship between sustainability and international trade. This complexity is highlighted in Roger Hayter's description of 'the war in the woods,' in which export-based resource exploitation faces conflict with environmental, cultural, and political imperatives. In resource peripheries, he argues, 'the post-Fordist transformation has featured complex interactions between industrial and resource dynamics in which powerful imperatives of flexibility, neoliberalism, environmentalism, and aboriginalism have clashed to contest industrial development and restructuring.' See Hayter, 'War in the Woods,' 707.
78 Ward et al., 'Regulation of Farm Pollution,' 1194–5; Blow, *Borrowed Time*; Barkin, 'Sustainability,' 8.
79 Waltner-Toews, 'Mad Cows,' 43.
80 Hildyard, 'Liberation Ecology,' 155.
81 Rees, 'Globalization and Sustainability,' 264.
82 Christiansen-Ruffman, 'Pages from Beijing,' 39.
83 Baxter and Mann, 'Survival and Revival,' 244; Leach and Winson, 'Globalization Down to Earth,' 346.
84 Kerr, 'Women's Rights,' 5, 7–9.
85 Shiva, 'Economic Globalization,' 22.
86 McMichael, 'Globalization'; Hessing, 'Women and Sustainability,' 20.
87 Pan, 'China's New Laborers,' 37.
88 Long and Kindon, 'Gender and Tourism Development,' 114.
89 Leach and Winson, 'Bringing Globalization Down to Earth,' 357.
90 Reed, 'Endangered Forests and Endangered Communities,' 120.
91 Cloke, 'State Deregulation,' 45.
92 Argent, 'Inside the Black Box,' 13; Bell and Cloke, 'Private and Public Sectors,' 3.
93 Argent, 'Inside the Black Box,' 13.
94 Marsden, 'Fordist Transition,' 221.

95 Jones and Tonts, 'Rural Restructuring,' 138.
96 Flora, 'Presidential Address,' 169.
97 Qualman, 'Corporate Hog Farming,' 28, 37
98 Bryden, 'Rural Renewal in Europe,' 6.
99 Nelson, 'Economic Restructuring,' 21.
100 Jones and Tonts, 'Rural Restructuring,' 138; Canadian Press, 'Rural Way of Life,' A13.
101 Mowforth and Munt, *Tourism and Sustainability*, 129.
102 Berry, 'Death of the Rural Community,' 183.

Chapter 3. Strategies for Sustainability

1 Livingstone, *Class Ideologies*, 179.
2 Wallerstein, 'Globalization or the Age of Transition?' 259.
3 Lipsey, Ragan, and Courant, *Microeconomics*, 31.
4 Habermas, *Knowledge and Human Interests*, 301.
5 Gregory, 'Existentialism,' 243.
6 Hall, 'Global Civil Society,' 11.
7 Gramsci, *Prison Notebooks*, 12.
8 Alan Bullock, 'Hegemony,' in Alan Bullock and Stephen Trombley (eds.), *New Fontana Dictionary of Modern Thought* (London: HarperCollins, 1999), 387–8.
9 Gramsci, *Prison Notebooks*, 12.
10 Ibid., 80.
11 In Entwistle, *Antonio Gramsci*, 15.
12 Gramsci, *Prison Notebooks*, 210.
13 Ibid., 12.
14 That force is clearly exposed in the violent police actions against peaceful protestors who have withdrawn their spontaneous consent to the hegemonic practices of supranational institutions such as the World Bank and the International Monetary Fund.
15 The Frankfurt School began in the 1920s as a group of German philosophers who adopted a form of social theory known as Critical Theory – 'a theory of history and society driven by a passionate commitment to understand how ideological systems and societal structures hinder and impede the fullest development of humankind's collective potential to be self-reflective and self-determining historical actor.' (Welton, *Defense of the Lifeworld*, 14). See also Habermas, *Theory of Communicative Action*, 2: 333; Habermas, *Philosophical Discourse of Modernity*, 315.
16 Michael Collins and Donovan Plumb, 'Some Critical Thinking about

Critical Theory and Its Relevance for Adult Education Practice.' Proceedings of the 30th Annual Education Research Conference, University of Wisconsin, Madison (1989), 98; Habermas, *Theory of Communicative Action*, 1: 322.

17 Connolly, 'Lifelong Learning through the Habermasian Lens,' 82; Habermas, *Theory of Communicative Action*, 1: 86.
18 Habermas, *Philosophical Discourse of Modernity*, 130.
19 Habermas, *Theory of Communicative Action*, 1: 100.
20 Habermas, *Theory of Communicative Action*, 2: 131.
21 Habermas, *Postmetaphysical Thinking*, 43.
22 Habermas, *Theory of Communicative Action*, 1: 100.
23 Ibid., 100–1.
24 Ibid., 342–3.
25 Habermas, *Theory of Communicative Action*, 2: 325.
26 Best and Kellner, *Postmodern Theory*, 239.
27 McMurtry, *Unequal Freedoms*, 298.
28 Ibid., 298.
29 Ibid., 299.
30 Ibid.
31 Ibid., 24.
32 McMurtry, *Cancer Stage of Capitalism*, 155.
33 McMurtry, *Unequal Freedoms*, 24.
34 Raymond Geuss, *The Idea of a Critical Theory: Habermas and the Frankfurt School* (Cambridge: Cambridge University Press, 1981), 75.
35 Bullock, 'Hegemony,' 388.
36 Holub, *Antonio Gramsci*, 6.
37 Entwistle, *Antonio Gramsci*, 4.
38 Lipson, *Great Issues of Politics*.
39 Buttel, 'Some Observations,' 265.
40 Robinson et al., 'Defining a Sustainable Society,' 44; Sewell, 'Seminar 2,' 38.
41 Röling and Wagemakers, *Facilitating Sustainable Agriculture*, 7.

Chapter 4. Searching for Sustainability: Past and Present

1 Woodgate and Redclift, 'Sociology of Nature,' 20.
2 Redclift, 'Sustainable Development,' 4; Simpson and Weiner, *Oxford English Dictionary*, 327; Merriam-Webster, *Webster's Ninth New Collegiate Dictionary* (Springfield, Mass.: Merriam-Webster, 1990), 1189. Gorman, Mehalik, and Werhane, *Ethical and Environmental Challenges*, 63.

3 Redclift, 'Sustainable Development,' 4.
4 See, for example, Troughton, 'Conflict or Sustainability,' 1, 11; Lee, 'Greed,' 563; Prugh, *Natural Capital,* 46; Farrell and Hart, 'What Does Sustainability Mean?,' 26; Bossel, *Indicators for Sustainable Development,* 2; Smailes, 'Sustainabile Rural Systems,' 101; Sachs, *Planet Dialectics,* 176; Prugh, Costanza, and Daly, *Local Politics,* 66.
5 See, for example, Richardson, 'What Is a "Sustainable City,"' 35; Norgaard, 'Sustainable Development,' 615.
6 See, for example, Siebenhüner, '*Homo sustinens,*' 19; Richardson, 'Sustainable City,' 35–6; Turner, *Sustainable Environmental Management,* 209; O'Riordan, 'Politics of Sustainability,' 30; Jayasuriya, 'Economists on Sustainability,' 232.
7 See, for example, Rosen, 'Sustainability,' 849; Emel, 'Sustainable Development,' 611; Kumar, Manning, and Murck. *Challenge of Sustainability,* 271.
8 See, for example, Peacock, 'Sustainability as Symbiosis,' 18–19; Peacock, 'Sustainability as Manifestation,' 9.
9 See, for example, Edwards, 'Sustainability Debate,' 230; Köhn et al., *Sustainability in Question,* 6; Röling and Wagemakers, *Facilitating Sustainable Agriculture,* 7.
10 See, for example, Redclift, *Sustainability,* 5; Köhn et al., *Sustainability in Question,* 9; O'Riordan, 'Politics of Sustainability,' 29.
11 See, for example, Woodgate and Redclift, 'Sociology of Nature,' 6; Pretty, *Regenerating Agriculture,* 11.
12 See, for example, Norgaard, 'Sustainable Development,' 614.
13 See, for example, O'Riordan, 'What Does Sustainability Mean?' 2, 8.
14 See, for example, Robinson et al., 'Defining a Sustainable Society,' 41, 44; Buttel, 'Some Observations,' 265; Richardson, 'Sustainable City,' 35; Yanarella and Levine, 1992. 'Sustainable Development,' 769.
15 Doob, *Sustainers and Sustainability,* ix.
16 Siebenhüner, '*Homo sustinens,*' 19.
17 O'Riordan, 'Politics of Sustainability,' 37; Buttel, 'Politics of Sustainability,' 261.
18 O'Riordan, 'Politics of Sustainability,' 29.
19 Farrell and Hart, 'What Does Sustainability Mean?,' 6.
20 Kane, 'Sustainability Concepts,' 15.
21 Simpson and Weiner, *OED,* 327; Sowell, *Say's Law,* 100; Buttel, 'Some Observations,' 263.
22 Talbot, 'World Conservation Strategy,' 495
23 Common, *Sustainability and Policy,* 4; see also Bossel, *Indicators for Sustainable Development,* 1.

24 O'Riordan, 'Politics of Sustainability,' 44–5; Redclift, 'Sustainable Development,' 5.

25 Meadows et al., *Limits to Growth*, 9, 11–12, 24, 158, 171.

26 Common, *Sustainability and Policy*, 2. It is interesting to note that the sequel to *The Limits to Growth*, entitled *Mankind at the Turning Point*, was a more upbeat, moderate interpretation of future outcomes and global sustainability. It could be argued that this second report to the Club of Rome represents yet one more way in which modern elites work out ways of coming through a crisis with their power intact.

27 WCED, 43, 46.

28 Ibid., 1.

29 Ibid., 40.

30 Ibid., 213.

31 Hunter, C., 'Sustainable Tourism,' 854–5.

32 Lohmann, 'Whose Common Future,' 82–4.

33 Rees, 'Ecology of Sustainable Development,' 18, 21.

34 Kane, 'Sustainability Concept,' 17. From an economic point of view, sustainable growth assumes some degree of substitutability. 'The basis of much of the conservationist criticism of economics may be rooted in the view that the majority of economists are believers in non-zero substitutability between natural and man-made capital' (Jayasuriya, 'Economists on Sustainability,' 237).

35 Conference Board of Canada, 'Corporate Social Responsibility,' CSR1–11.

36 Jayasuriya, 'Economists on Sustainability,' 231.

37 Farrell and Hart, 'What Does Sustainability Mean,' 30.

38 Jayasuriya, 'Economists on Sustainability,' 232.

39 Brown et al., 'Global Sustainability,' 16; Köhn et al., *Sustainability in Question*, 9.

40 Röling and Wagemakers, *Facilitating Sustainable Agriculture*, 9; Worster, 'Shaky Ground,' 420; Richardson, 'Sustainable City,' 36.

41 Kane, 'Sustainability Concepts,' 19.

42 Goodstein, *Economics and the Environment*, 81.

43 Brown et al., 'Global Sustainability,' 716. See also Pezzey, 'Definitions of Sustainability,' 15, 16.

44 Neoliberalism is a set of economic policies that includes the rule of the market, cutting public expenditure for social services, deregulation, and privatization and eliminating the concept of 'the public good' or 'community' (Martinez and Garcia, 'What Is "Neo-Liberalism,"' 419).

45 Prugh, Costanza, and Daly, *Local Politics*, 71; Kane, 'Sustainability Concepts,' 22.

46 In Pezzey, 'Definitions of Sustainability,' 16; Conference Board of Canada, 'Corporate Social Responsibility,' CSR1–11.

47 Utility is the satisfaction or pleasure a person derives from the consumption

of a good or service. In the context used by economists, utility is not a *prop-erty* of a good or service, but the derivation of satisfaction from the *use* of such a good or service (Pass et al., *HarperCollins Dictionary of Economics*, 539). Utility theory is the basis of neoclassical economics, which rests on the doc-trine of consumer sovereignty and an ideological belief in both individualism and libertarianism – that individuals are the best judges of their own needs (Johnston, 'Utility Theory,' 666); Pezzey, 'Definitions of Sustainability,' 19, 24.

48 Goodstein, *Economics and the Environment*, 81.
49 Brown et al., 'Global Sustainability,' 717.
50 Rees, 'Globalization and Sustainability,' 259.
51 Köhn et al., *Sustainability in Question*, 3; Goodstein, *Economics and the Environment*, 109.
52 Brown et al., 'Global Sustainability,' 716.
53 Worster, 'Shaky Ground,' 419.
54 Farrell and Hart, 'What Does Sustainability Mean,' 7; Robinson et al., 'Defining a Sustainable Society,' 44; Redclift, 'Multiple Dimensions,' 37.
55 Brown et al., 'Global Sustainability,' 716.
56 Rees, 'More Jobs, Less Damage,' 26. Redclift, 'Sustainable Development,' 18–19; Buttel, 'Some Observations,' 268.
57 Drummond and Marsden, *Condition of Sustainability*, 7–8; Brown et al., 'Global Sustainability,' 716.
58 Although dialogically oriented, PRA does not always meet dialogical expec-tations. In an appraisal of PRA, von Kotze (1998) questions whether it promotes 'monologues or dialogues.' Writing from a Freirian perspective, she argues that dialogue involves more than the simple role reversal in-volved in PRA: 'Dialogue implies critical reflection, the belief in the power to transform reality through collective action, and the will to do so' (53).
59 Prugh, Costanza, and Daly, *Local Politics*, 2.
60 Rees, 260.
61 Worster, 'Shaky Ground,' 424.

Chapter 5. Searching for Sustainability: Future

1 Prugh, Costanza, and Daly, *Local Politics*, 41.
2 Cerny, 'Globalization and the Changing Logic,' 112–13.
3 Roddick, 'WTO's Charm Offensive,' 15. Owner of the Body Shop, Roddick not only marched in Seattle and criticizes the WTO and the IMF, but community-trades with a sesame farmers' co-operative, sustaining their livelihood and culture after the price for sesame crashed in 1993.
4 Cerny, 'Changing Logic,' 113.

5 Yanarella and Levine, 'Sustainable Development,' 769; Rasmussen, in Prugh, Costanza, and Daly, *Local Politics*, 4; Sewell, 'Seminar 2,' 37–8; Röling and Wagemakers, *Facilitating Sustainable Agriculture*, 9.

6 Prugh, Costanza, and Daly, *Local Politics*, 108.

7 Ibid., 113.

8 McMurtry, 'Global Development,' 1.

9 McMurtry, *Unequal Freedoms*, 24.

10 McMurtry, 'Corporate Male Gang,' 835.

11 McMurtry, *Cancer Stage of Capitalism*, 217.

12 McMurtry, *Unequal Freedoms*, 371.

13 McMurtry, *Cancer Stage of Capitalism*, 215.

14 McMurtry, *Unequal Freedoms*, 25.

15 Ibid., 216.

16 Ibid., 376, 371.

17 McMurtry, *Cancer Stage of Capitalism*, 52.

18 McMurtry, *Unequal Freedoms*, 377.

19 Mark Neufeld, 'Theorizing Globalization: Towards a Politics of Resistance.' Trent International Political Economy Centre working paper, Trent University, Peterborough, Ont. (2001): 8. www.trentu.ca/tipec. Campbell concurs, arguing that structural adjustment programs put forward by the World Bank included policies of state withdrawal from 'involvement in productive economic activities in order to leave the operations of the market as free as possible' ('New Rules of the Game,' 12). However, in the face of social collapse caused by these SAPs, the World Bank now feels that 'an effective state is vital for the provision of goods and services – and the rules and institutions – that allow markets to flourish' (13). In other words, corporate globalization now needs the state to help enforce and promote its neoliberal economic policies.

20 McMurtry, *Cancer Stage of Capitalism*, 217, 88, 213.

21 Ibid., 88. These social immune systems include laws, statutes, and rules to ensure the purity of food, milk and water supplies, and handlers; the construction and maintenance of community systems of waste and garbage disposal; the systematic testing, inspecting, and screening of commercial pharmaceuticals and other non-food products to validate their safety for human use and consumption; the formation of administrative and liability norms to protect workers' health and safety in their places of employment; and the provision of public centres, clinics, and hospitals to administer tests, inoculations, and curative care free of charge (86–7).

22 OMAFRA, '2001–2002 Business Plan'; Salutin, 'Walkerton,' A15. In 2000, after years of neoliberal restructuring, cutbacks, tax credits, and infrastruc-

ture decimation, the water in the rural community of Walkerton, Ontario, became contaminated with E-coli bacteria. Seven people died and hundreds were made sick.

23 McMurtry, *Cancer Stage of Capitalism*, 213, 214.

24 Benton, 'Biology and Social Theory,' 41.

25 As a result of such 'cost saving,' Wachtel (*Poverty of Affluence*, 150) reports that epidemiological studies have concluded that environmental factors cause from 70 to 90 per cent of all cancers.

26 Harvey, 'Between Space and Time,' 422–3.

27 An exception is certified organic products, although many large corporate players in the organic market are adhering to the letter, but not the spirit, of certification (itself a form of the civil commons), or are attempting to set up their own set of regulations that will allow them to bypass strict environmental regulations.

28 Lauzon, *Exploring the Foundations*, 88–9, 90, 91. One example of such an alienated view of the world, reported by Lee (1993, 562), is that 'trees may grow faster in bank accounts than they do in the woods.' In other words, 'harvesting populations at unsustainable speed, mining the resource, can be rational if the earnings from harvest produce financial assets whose value appreciates more rapidly than the resource would regenerate.'

29 In McMurtry, *Cancer Stage of Capitalism*, 159.

30 Ibid., 156, 157.

31 Ibid., 160.

32 Redclift, 'Sustainability and Sociology.'

33 Sachs, 'Social Sustainability,' 30; Allen and Sachs, 'Social Side of Sustainability,' 575; Redclift, 'Sustainability and Sociology,' 71; Brecher, Costello, and Smith, *Globalization from Below*, 11; Barlow, *Free Trade Area*.

34 This means that sustainability is ultimately a human issue, not an environmental issue. It entails human action towards the environment, not the environment itself. The environment is/provides life goods to an innumerable range of species, including the human species, and so must be protected by the cooperative human construct of the civil commons. In this way, sustainability protects the civil commons, which in turn protects the environment.

35 McMurtry, *Cancer Stage of Capitalism*, 216.

36 Clark, K. 'Top 10 Things Wrong,' 9–12.

37 McMurtry, *Unequal Freedoms*, 380.

38 Brecher, Costello, and Smith, *Globalization from Below*, 10, 16.

39 McMurtry, *Unequal Freedoms*, 391.

40 Ibid., 393.

41 Wiebe, 'Afterword,' 327. In the words of the editors of this book, 'the

countryside is coming to serve two new and very different purposes – playground and dumping ground' (xv).

42 The Crow rate (named after the Crowsnest Pass Agreement) was implemented in 1897 as a concession by the Canadian Pacific Railway to reduce freight rates, particularly on cereal crops. The loss of the Crow rate, which for almost a century had underwritten the shipping costs of export grain production, had 'widespread and deeply felt impacts that significantly affect the economic landscapes of the prairies.' In Ramsey and Everitt, 'Post-Crow Farming,' 4.

43 McMurtry, *Unequal Freedoms*, 381.

44 Osha Gray Davidson, *Broken Heartland: The Rise of America's Rural Ghetto* (Iowa City: University of Iowa Press, 1996), 168–9.

45 McMurtry, *Unequal Freedoms*, 399.

46 McMurtry, *Cancer Stage of Capitalism*, 205.

47 Hardin, 'Tragedy of the Commons,' 1245.

48 Röling, 'Idea Called Knowledge System.'

49 Mies and Bennholdt-Thomsen, *Subsistence Perspective*, 156, 157.

50 Feeny et al., 'Tragedy of the Commons,' 1.

51 Finger and Asún, *Adult Education*, 163–4.

52 Ibid., 169.

53 McHattie, 'Resistance of Farmers,' 163. Resistance has a long history and can take many forms, from low-level obstructions in the workplace to full-blown armed insurrections within and between nations. Politically based, resistance involves opposition to domination and oppression. Rural resistance, like other forms of resistance, is complex and contested. Groups of stakeholders can find themselves allying or competing with other groups of stakeholders in a fluid manner, depending on the issue involved. For example, the resistance to old-growth logging in the Clayquot Sound area of British Columbia involved alliances between urban-based environmentalists and local First Nations groups, while many residents of rural logging communities sided with the multinational giants. These same residents might find themselves opposing the logging corporations on other issues, such as working conditions or mill closures. At the community level, some argue that communities are powerless in the face of global forces, while others maintain that there is considerable room for local resistance, especially where communities have the collective will to negotiate with external interests. See Mackenzie and Norcliffe, 'Restructuring,' 3.

54 Paula Allman, *Revolutionary Social Transformation: Democratic Hopes, Political Possibilities and Critical Education* (Westport, Conn.: Bergin and Garvey, 1999), 9.

55 Cox, 'Market as God.'

56 Some might argue that the civil commons already plays a more central role in society than many people realize. Hilkka Pietila has analysed the Finnish economy into three spheres and calculated the proportion of time spent and value created in each. The Free Economy, made up of all non-monetary production for local use, accounted for 54% of total work time and 35% of total value of production. The Protected Economy, which includes all production for the home market, including such services as transportation, health, and education, accounted for 36% of work time and 46% of value. The Fettered Economy, which is production for international exchange, accounted for only 10% of the work time and 19% of value of production (in Miles 'Learning from the Women's Movement,' 255).

57 McMurtry, 'Education and the Market Model,' 209.

58 The General Agreement on Trade in Services (GATS), put forward by the World Trade Organization, sees public funding as a subsidy, and will treat subsidies as unfair competition or barriers to entry for foreign services and suppliers. This will massively reduce, and could end, public-sector funding (Sanders 'GATS,' 6). Since much of the civil commons is based on public-sector funding, this corporate fiat poses enormous challenges for the future of the civil commons.

59 McMurtry, *Cancer Stage of Capitalism*, 163.

60 Sherri Torjman, 'Education and the Public Good,' Caledon Institute of Social Policy, Communities and Schools Series (April 2000): 3. http://www.caledoninst.org.

61 Lauzon and Leahy, 'Educational Reform,' 40.

62 Nader, 'Stop Americanizing Medicare,' 12.

63 Gro Harlem Brundtland, former chair of the World Commission on Environment and Development and current director-general of the World Health Organization, provides a telling example of the growing influence of the money values of corporate health care. A recent speech to business leaders, bankers, and heads of state made it clear that Dr Brundtland considers access to health care not as a right but as a means to increase productivity (Motchane, 'WHO's Responsible,' 11).

64 According to Sanders ('GATS,' 6), in line with the 'progressive liberalisation' that lies at the heart of all WTO agreements, the GATS involves regular rounds of negotiation where governments progressively negotiate away their regulatory authority with no backtracking allowed between rounds. Governments have a single opportunity to list their market-access restrictions when they first sign up to the GATS. These restrictions are the main bargaining chips traded off in the negotiation process, which

pressures governments to increase the number of service sectors they will expose in each successive round. The eventual outcome will be no restrictions, even in areas such as health care.

65 McMurtry, *Unequal Freedoms*, 25.
66 While universal access is crucial to any instantiation of the civil commons, health care also serves many other functions that are linked to sustainability. For example, the rural hospital, as the centre of rural health care, is 'not just vital to the health of individuals within the community, but is vital to the economic, social and environmental health and well-being of the community as a whole' (Lauzon and Hagglund, 'From the Ground Up,' 20).

Chapter 6. New Directions for Research

1 O'Riordan, 'Politics of Sustainability,' 30.
2 Shearman, 'Meaning and Ethics,' 2.
3 Hardoy, Mitlin, and Satterthwaite, *Environmental Problems in Third World Cities*, 172. Sustainable development, however, is not as popular as some would like to think. A recent survey by Entec found that 45 per cent of directors and chief executives of major businesses across the UK had never heard of sustainable development (*Ecologist*, 'Notes,' 11).
4 Daly, 'Operational Principles,' 1.
5 McMurtry, *Value Wars*, 177.
6 Silver, 'Drive to Globalization,' 31.
7 Mark Roseland, *Toward Sustainable Communities: A Resource Book for Municipal and Local Governments* (Ottawa: National Round Table on the Environment and the Economy, 1992), 215–16; Mark Roseland, *Toward Sustainable Communities: Resources for Citizens and Their Governments* (Gabriola Island, B.C.: New Society Publishers, 1998), 160.
8 WCED, *Our Common Future*, 43.
9 Ellwood, 'Stop Ransacking the Earth,' 10. For example, the corporate giant Unilever Foods was prepared to commit to sustainable development, but required a definition of sustainable development that was not only meaningful in their everyday business but also supported the new Corporate Purpose (Gorman, Mehalik, and Werhane, *Ethical and Environmental Challenges*, 159).
10 Reid, *Sustainable Development*, 65.
11 Buttel, 'Some Observations,' 264; Barkin, 'Sustainability,' 24.
12 Fuller, Ehrensaft, and Gertler, 'Sustainable Rural Communities,' 30.
13 Daly, 'World Simply Can't,' 22.

14 In Lohmann, 'Whose Common Future,' 83; Kumar, Manning, and Murck, *Challenge of Sustainability*, 271.

15 Day, 'Working With the Grain,' 102.

16 Jones and Tonts, 'Rural Restructuring,' 136.

17 Cloke, 'Rural Community,' 718.

18 Bridger and Harp, 'Ideology and Growth Promotion,' 269. This finding is part of the growth machine hypothesis, which argues that 'the local elites who most vigorously promote growth are those most likely to reap the benefits: local businessmen, particularly property owners and investors in locally oriented financial institutions; lawyers; syndicators, and realtors ... Although these elites may be divided on other issues, growth ... is the one goal around which all important groups can rally. The more financially powerful members of the locality thus form what may be thought of as a growth machine ... [which] typically operates by attempting ... to use government to gain those resources which enhance the growth potential of the locality' (269).

19 Duncan and Lamborghini, 'Poverty and Social Context,' 458–9.

20 Ibid., 438.

21 Fuller, Ehrensaft, and Gertler, 'Sustainable Rural Communities,' 30.

22 Bryden, 'Some Preliminary Perspectives,' 48; Bridger and Luloff, 'Toward an Interactional Approach,' 381; Hart, Maureen, 'Sustainability.'

23 Berry, *Sex, Economy, Freedom*, 14.

24 Scott, Park, and Cocklin, 'Sustainable Rural Communities,' 443.

25 Beveridge, 1996. 'Globalization and Sustainability,' 70.

26 Sklair, 'Social Movements,' 520, 524. In a jawdropping but convincing explanation, Sklair argues that, in one sense, shopping is the most successful social movement, since it is 'the second most important leisure-time activity in the USA (after watching TV, and much of TV promotes shopping anyway),' 531.

27 George, 'How to Win.'

28 The role of a supranational institution such as the International Monetary Fund as one of the structures that builds corporate globalization is made clear in the words of its 1983 report: 'The major shift ... from capital to labour that took place in the late 1960s and early 1970s has not been fully reversed and remains an important factor accounting for low profitability and low investment' (Kolko, *Restructuring the World Economy*, 46).

29 Held, 'Regulating Globalization,' 403, 404.

30 Prugh, Costanza, and Daly, *Local Politics*, 61.

31 Bishop, 'Sustaining Community,' 23.

32 McMurtry, *Unequal Freedoms*, 370.
33 Laxer, 'Radical Transformative Nationalisms,' 148.
34 Sklair, 'Social Movements,' 534.
35 Ibid.
36 Style, 'Gustavo Esteva,' 22.
37 Ibid., 140.
38 One exception is the European Union, but even its supranational provision
    of life goods is under threat. Under the terms of the Maastricht Treaty, the
    fiscal policy of all governments in the European Union is now prescribed by
    a central formula, including the reduction of social spending, and control
    of money and credit policies has been transferred to a European Central
    Bank that is accountable to no electoral or other body but itself (McMurtry,
    Unequal Freedoms, 253–4, fn. 28).
39 Buttel, 'Some Observations,' 273; Barlow, Interview.
40 Marsden, 'Exploring a Rural Sociology,' 219.
41 Salamon and Tornatore, 'Territory Contested,' 639.

Bibliography

Adams, W.M. *Green Development: Environment and Sustainability in the Third World.*
  New York: Routledge, 1990.
Adbusters. 'Act Locally.' 2001. http://adbusters.org/campaigns/corporate/
  actlocally.
– 'Rest in Peace.' 34 (March–April 2001): 35.
Albrecht, D.E. 'The Industrial Transformation of Farm Communities: Implica-
  tions for Family Structure and Socioeconomic Conditions.' *Rural Sociology* 63,
  no. 1 (1998): 51–64.
Albrow, Martin. 'Globalization.' In William Outhwaite and Tom Bottomore
  (eds.), *The Blackwell Dictionary of Twentieth-Century Social Thought.* Cambridge,
  Mass.: Blackwell, 1993.
Allen, Patricia L., and Carolyn E. Sachs. 'The Social Side of Sustainability: Class,
  Gender and Race.' *Science as Culture* 2 (1991): 569–90.
Altieri, Miguel A. 'Sustainable Agriculture.' In Charles J. Arntzen (ed.), *Encyclo-
  pedia of Agricultural Science.* Vol. 4. Toronto: Academic Press, 1994.
Argent, N. 'Inside the Black Box: Dimensions of Gender, Generation and Scale
  in the Australian Rural Restructuring Process.' *Journal of Rural Studies* 15, no.
  1 (1999): 1–15.
Arnstein, Sherry R. 'A Ladder of Citizen Participation.' *Journal of the American
  Institute of Planners* 35, no. 4 (1969): 216–24.
Bailey, Clayton. 'Where Have All the People Gone?' *Guardian Weekly* (27 June–
  3 July 2002): 22.
Bairoch, Paul. 'The Constituent Economic Principles of Globalization in Historical Perspective: Myths and Realities.' *International Sociology* 15, no. 2 (June,
  2000): 197–214.
Barkin, D. 'Sustainability: The Political Economy of Autonomous Develop-
  ment.' *Organization and Environment* 11, no. 1 (1998): 5–32.

Barlow, Maude. Interview on CPAC, 5 November 1999.

– *The Free Trade Area of the Americas and the Threat to Social Programs, Environmental Sustainability and Social Justice in Canada and the Americas.* The Council of Canadians (18 January 2001). http://www.canadians.org.

Barnes, Trevor J., and Roger Hayter. '"The Little Town That Did": Flexible Accumulation and Community Response in Chemainus, British Columbia.' *Regional Studies* 26, no. 7 (1992): 647–63.

Baxter, V., and S. Mann. 'The Survival and Revival of Non-Wage Labour in a Global Economy.' *Sociologia Ruralis* 32, no. 2/3, (1992): 231–47.

Beckett, Andy. 'When Corporate Love Just Isn't Cool.' *Guardian Weekly* (15–21 March 2001): 16.

Bell, P., and P. Cloke. 'The Changing Relationship between the Private and Public Sectors: Privatisation and Rural Britain.' *Journal of Rural Studies* 5, no. 1 (1989): 1–15.

Benton, Ted. 'Biology and Social Theory in the Environmental Debate.' In Ted Benton and Michael Redclift (eds.), *Social Theory and the Global Environment.* New York: Routledge, 1994.

Berry, Wendell. *Sex, Economy, Freedom and Community.* New York: Pantheon Books, 1993.

– 'Conserving Communities.' In Jerry Mander and Edward Goldsmith (eds.), *The Case against the Global Economy – And for a Turn Toward the Local.* San Francisco: Sierra Club Books, 1996.

– 'The Death of the Rural Community.' *Ecologist* 29, no. 3 (1999): 183–4.

Best, Stephen, and Douglas Kellner. *Postmodern Theory: Critical Interrogations.* New York: Guilford Press, 1991.

Beveridge, Dan. 'Globalization and Sustainability: Issues and Options for Adult Education.' *Convergence* 29, no. 4 (1996): 68–75.

Bhagwati, Jagdish. 'Coping with Antiglobalization: A Trilogy of Discontents.' *Foreign Affairs* 81, no. 1 (2002): 2–7.

Bishop, Mary. 'Sustaining Community in Rural Canada.' *Plan Canada* 40, no. 1 (1999–2000): 23.

Blackmore, Jill. 'Warning Signals or Dangerous Opportunities? Globalization, Gender, and Educational Policy Shifts.' *Educational Theory* 50, no. 4 (2000): 467–86.

Blanc, M. 'Family Farming in a Changing World.' *Sociologia Ruralis* 34, no. 4 (1994): 279–92.

Blow, P. *Borrowed Time.* 49 North Productions, TVOntario, 1990. Videocassette.

Bossel, Hartmut. *Indicators for Sustainable Development: Theory, Method, Applications.* Winnipeg, Man.: International Institute for Sustainable Development, 1999.

Brecher, Jeremy, John Brown Childs, and Jill Cutler, eds. *Global Visions: Beyond the New World Order*. Boston: South End Press, 1993.

Brecher, Jeremy, and Tim Costello. *Global Village or Global Pillage: Economic Reconstruction from the Bottom Up*. Boston: South End Press, 1994.

Brecher, Jeremy, Tim Costello, and Brendan Smith. *Globalization from Below: The Power of Solidarity*. Boston: South End Press, 2000.

Breheny, M. 'Towards Sustainable Urban Development.' In A. Mannion and S. Bowlby (eds.), *Environmental Issues in the 1990s*. London: John Wiley and Sons, 1992.

Bridger, Jeffrey C., and Aaron J. Harp. 'Ideology and Growth Promotion.' *Journal of Rural Studies* 6, no. 3 (1990): 269–77.

Bridger, Jeffrey C., and A.E. Luloff. 'Toward an Interactional Approach to Sustainable Community Development.' *Journal of Rural Studies* 15 (1999): 377–87.

Bridgwater, William, and Seymour Kurtz, eds. *Columbia Encyclopedia*. 3d ed. New York: Columbia University Press, 1963.

Brittain, V., and L. Elliott. 'World's Poor Lose Out to Corporations.' *Guardian Weekly* (22 June 1997).

Brown, Becky J., Mark E. Hanson, Diana M. Liverman, and Robert W. Merideth, Jr. 'Global Sustainability: Toward Definition.' *Environmental Management* 11, no. 6 (1987): 713–19.

Brown, David L. 'Demographic Trends Relevant to Education in Nonmetro America.' Paper presented at the Rural Education Symposium, Washington, DC (30 March 1987). ERIC Accession No. ED283666.

Brummer, Alex. 'Globalization.' In Alan Bullock and Stephen Trombley (eds.), *New Fontana Dictionary of Modern Thought*. London: HarperCollins, 1999.

Bryden, John. 'Some Preliminary Perspectives on Sustainable Rural Communities.' In John Bryden (ed.), *Towards Sustainable Rural Communities: The Guelph Seminar Series*. Guelph, Ontario: University School of Rural Planning and Development, 1994.

– 'Rural Renewal in Europe: Global Tendencies and Local Responses.' *Leader Magazine* 18 (autumn 1998): 4–12.

Bullock, Alan. 'Hegemony.' In Alan Bullock and Stephen Trombley (eds.) *New Fontana Dictionary of Modern Thought*. London: HarperCollins, 1999. 387–8.

Bullock, Alan, and Stephen Trombley, eds. *Fontana Dictionary of Modern Thought*. London: Fontana Press, 1988.

Buttel, Frederick H. 'Some Observations on States, World Orders, and the Politics of Sustainability.' *Organization and Environment* 11, no. 3 (1998): 261–86.

Bygrave, Mike. 'Where Have All the Protesters Gone?' *Guardian Weekly* (1–7 August 2002): 21.

CCPA Monitor, 'The Corporate Takeover of the United Nations Continues' (September 1998): 24–5.

Campbell, Bonnie. 'New Rules of the Game: The World Bank's Role in the Construction of New Normative Frameworks for States, Markets and Social Exclusion.' *Canadian Journal of Development Studies* 21, no. 1 (2000): 7–30.

Canadian Press. 'Rural Way of Life at Stake, Farmers Say.' *Globe and Mail.* 5 December 1998.

Carr, Barry. Globalization from Below: Labour Internationalism under NAFTA. *International Social Science Journal* 51, no. 1 (1999): 49–59.

Carroll, W.K., and R.S. Ratner. 'Between Leninism and Radical Pluralism: Gramscian Reflections on Counter-Hegemony and the New Social Movements.' *Critical Sociology* 20, no. 2, (1994): 3–26.

Cary, John. 'Lessons from Past and Present Attempts to Develop Sustainable Land Use Systems.' *Review of Marketing and Agricultural Economics* 60, no. 2 (1992): 277–84.

Cassidy, J. 'The Return of Karl Marx.' *New Yorker.* 20–7 October 1997, 248–59.

Cerny, Philip G. 'Globalization and the Changing Logic of Collective Action.' In Charles Lipson and Benjamin J. Cohen (eds.), *Theory and Structure in International Political Economy.* Cambridge, Mass.: MIT Press, 1999.

Christiansen-Ruffman, Linda. 'Pages from Beijing.' *Canadian Woman Studies* 16, no. 3 (1996): 35–43.

Ciccantell, P.S. 'Globalization, Restructuring, and Hard Times in Three Raw Materials-Dependent Communities.' Paper presented at the American Sociological Association, Cambridge, Mass., 1999. Cambridge Scientific Abstracts Accession Number 99S38029.

Clark, E. Ann. 'Ten Reasons Why Farmers Should Think Twice before Growing GE Crops.' 2001. www.oac.uoguelph.ca/www/CRSC/faculty/eac/ 10reasons.htm.

Clark, Karen. 'The Top 10 Things Wrong with Environmental Protection under the Common Sense Revolution.' *Intervenor* 25, nos. 3, 4 (2000): 9–12.

Clark, Mary E. 'Integrating Human Needs into Our Vision of Sustainability.' *Futures,* 26, no. 2 (1994): 180–4.

Cloke, Paul. 'State Deregulation and New Zealand's Agricultural Sector.' *Sociologia Ruralis* 29, no. 1 (1989): 34–47.

– 'Rural.' In R.J. Johnston, Derek Gregory, and David M. Smith (eds.), *Dictionary of Human Geography.* 3rd. ed. Malden, Mass.: Blackwell, 1998.

– 'Rural Community.' In R.J. Johnston, Derek Gregory, Geraldine Pratt, and Michael Watts (eds.), *Dictionary of Human Geography.* 4th ed. Malden, Mass.: Blackwell, 2000.

Coates, Ken. 'Northland: The Past, Present, and Future of Northern British Columbia in an Age of Globalization.' In Roger Epp and Dave Whitson (eds.), *Writing Off the Rural West: Globalization, Governments, and the Transformation of Rural Communities.* Edmonton: University of Alberta Press, 2001.

Coben, Diana. 'Revisiting Gramsci.' *Studies in the Education of Adults* 27, no. 1 (1995): 36–51.

– *Radical Heroes: Gramsci, Freire and the Politics of Adult Education.* New York: Garland, 1998.

Common, Michael. *Sustainability and Policy: Limits to Economics.* New York: Cambridge University Press, 1995.

Conference Board of Canada. 'Taking Corporate Social Responsibility to the Next Level.' *Maclean's* 113, no. 20 (15 May 2000): CSR1–11.

Connolly, Brian. 'Lifelong Learning through the Habermasian Lens: Providing a Theoretical Grounding to Adult Education Practice.' Lifelong Learning: Reality, Rhetoric and Public Policy Conference proceedings, University of Surrey, Guildford, England (4–6 July), 1997.

Cox, Harvey. 'The Market as God: Living in the New Dispensation.' *Atlantic Monthly* (March 1999): 18–23.

Dahms, F. and J. McComb. '"Counterurbanization," Interaction and Functional Change in a Rural Amenity Area - A Canadian Example.' *Journal of Rural Studies,* 15, no. 2 (1999): 129–46.

Daly, Herman E. 'Toward Some Operational Principles of Sustainable Development.' *Ecological Economics* 2 (1990): 1–6.

– 'Globalization versus Internationalization - Some Implications.' *Ecological Economics* 31 (1999): 31–7.

– 'World Simply Can't Grow Its Way Out of Poverty, Pollution.' *CCPA Monitor* (April 2001).

Daniels, Steven E., and Gregg B. Walker. 'Collaborative Learning: Improving Public Deliberation in Ecosystem-based Management.' *Environmental Impact Assessment Review* 16 (1996): 71–102.

Davidson, Osha Gray. *Broken Heartland: The Rise of America's Rural Ghetto.* Iowa City: University of Iowa Press, 1996.

Day, Graham. 'Working With the Grain? Towards Sustainable Rural and Community Development.' *Journal of Rural Studies* 14, no. 1 (1998): 89–105.

De la Court, Thijs. *Beyond Brundtland: Green Development in the 1990s.* Trans. Ed Bayens and Nigel Harle. New York: New Horizons Press, 1990.

Dollar, David, and Aart Kraay. 'Spreading the Wealth.' *Foreign Affairs* 81, no. 1 (2002): 120–33.

Doob, Leonard, W. *Sustainers and Sustainability: Attitudes, Attributes and Actions for Survival.* Westport, Conn.: Praeger, 1995.

Drache, D. ed. *Staples, Markets, and Cultural Change: Selected Essays, Harold A. Innis.* Montreal and Kingston: McGill-Queen's University Press, 1995.

Drache, D. and M.S. Gertler, eds. *The New Era of Global Competition: State Policy and Market Power.* Montreal: McGill-Queen's University Press, 1991.

Drummond, Ian, and Terry Marsden. *The Condition of Sustainability.* New York: Routledge, 1999.

Dryzek, John S. 'Global Ecological Democracy.' In Nicholas Low (ed.), *Global Ethics and Environment.* New York: Routledge, 1999.

Duncan, C.M. 'Understanding Persistent Poverty: Social Class Context in Rural Communities.' *Rural Sociology* 61, no. 1 (1996): 103–24.

Duncan, C.M., and N. Lamborghini. 'Poverty and Social Context in Remote Rural Communities.' *Rural Sociology* 59, no. 3 (1994): 437–61.

Ecologist, 'Notes.' March 2001. 11.

Economist, 'Today's Pig Is Tomorrow's Bacon.' 22 April 2000.

– 'The Case for Globalization.' 23 September 2000.

Edwards, Geoff. 'The Sustainability Debate: Has It Affected Our Way of Thinking and Our Policy Advice? Convenor's Introduction.' *Review of Marketing and Agricultural Economics* 60, no. 2 (1992): 227–30.

Eller, Ron, and Timothy Collins. 'Emerging Issue 3: Characteristics of Self-Sustaining Communities.' Appalachian Center, University of Kentucky. 2001. http://www.uky.edu/RGS/AppalCenter/arc_iss3.htm.

Elliott, Larry. 'A World Driven by Blind Greed.' *Guardian Weekly* (July 1999): 15–21.

– 'Making Globalisation Work for World's Poor.' *Guardian Weekly* (29 June – 5 July 2000), 14.

Ellwood, Wayne. 'Let's Stop Ransacking the Earth and Start Searching for Sustainability.' *New Internationalist,* no. 329 (November 2000): 9–12.

– *The No-Nonsense Guide to Globalization.* Toronto: New Internationalist Publications Ltd. and Between the Lines, 2001.

Emel, Jody. 'Sustainable Development.' In R.J. Johnston, Derek Gregory, and David M. Smith (eds.), *Dictionary of Human Geography.* 3d ed. Malden, Mass.: Blackwell, 1994.

Encyclopaedia Britannica. s.v. 'Utopia.' http://www.britannica.com.

Entwistle, Harold. *Antonio Gramsci: Conservative Schooling for Radical Politics.* Boston: Routledge and Kegan Paul, 1979.

Epp, Roger and Dave Whitson, eds. *Writing Off the Rural West: Globalization, Governments, and the Transformation of Rural Communities.* Edmonton: University of Alberta Press, 2001.

Falk, Ian, and Sue Kilpatrick. 'What *Is* Social Capital? A Study of Interaction in a Rural Community.' *Sociologia Ruralis* 40, no. 1 (2000): 87–110.

Falk, Richard. 'The Making of Global Citizenship.' In Jeremy Brecher, John
    Brown Childs, and Jill Cutler (eds.) *Global Visions: Beyond the New World Order.*
    Boston: South End Press, 1993.

Farrell, Alex, and Maureen Hart. 'What Does Sustainability Really Mean? The
    Search for Useful Indicators.' *Environment* 40, no. 9 (1998): 4–9, 26–31.

Feeny, David, Fikret Berkes, Bonnie J. McCay, and James M. Acheson. 'The
    Tragedy of the Commons: Twenty-Two Years Later.' *Human Ecology* 18, no. 1
    (1990).

Finger, Matthias, and José Manuel Asún. *Adult Education at the Crossroads: Learn-
    ing Our Way Out.* London: Zed Books, 2001.

Flora, Cornelia Butler. 'Presidential Address: Rural Peoples in a Global Econ-
    omy.' *Rural Sociology* 55, no. 2 (1990): 157–77.

Flora, Cornelia Butler, and Jan L. Flora. 'Entrepreneurial Social Infrastructure:
    A Necessary Ingredient.' *The Annals of the American Academy of Political and
    Social Science* 529 (September 1993): 48–58.

Fogal, C. 'Globalization and Sovereignty.' Presentation to the World Order
    Conference, Toronto, 4 June 1999.

Foley, Griff. 'Adult Education and Capitalist Reorganisation.' *Studies in the
    Education of Adults* 26, no. 2 (1994): 121–45.

Freire, Paulo. *Pedagogy of Hope.* New York: Continuum, 1995.

– *Pedagogy of the Oppressed.* New York: Continuum, 1996.

Freudenburg, William R. 'Addictive Economies: Extractive Industries and
    Vulnerable Localities in a Changing World Economy.' *Rural Sociology* 57, no. 3
    (1992): 305–32.

Friedmann, John. *Empowerment: The Politics of Alternative Development.* Cambridge
    Mass.: Blackwell, 1995.

Fromm, Erich. *The Art of Loving.* New York: Harper and Row, 1967.

Fuller, Tony, Philip Ehrensaft, and Michael Gertler. 'Sustainable Rural Commu-
    nities in Canada: Issues and Prospects.' In Michael E. Gertler and Harold R.
    Baker (eds.), *Proceedings of Rural Policy Seminar No. 1: Sustainable Rural Commu-
    nities in Canada* (Saskatoon, Sask. 11–13 October 1989). Saskatoon: Canadian
    Agriculture and Rural Restructuring Group, 1990. 1–41.

Gaventa, J. 'From the Mountains to the Maquiladoras: A Case Study of Capital
    Flight and Its Impact on Workers.' In J. Gaventa, B. Smith, and A. Willingham
    (eds.) *Communities in Economic Crisis.* Philadelphia: Temple University Press,
    1990. 85–95.

George, Susan. 'How to Win the War of Ideas: Lessons from the Gramscian
    Right.' *Dissent* 44, no. 3 (1997). http://www.igc.apc.org/dissent/archive/
    summer97/george.html.

– 'Power in the New World Order.' *Monetary Reform Magazine* (fall 1997): 10–20.

– 'A Short History of Neo-liberalism: Twenty Years of Elite Economics and Emerging Opportunities for Structural Change.' Paper presented at the Conference on Economic Sovereignty in a Globalising World. Bangkok, 24–6 March, 1999. http://www.millennium-round.org/Susan%20George.html.
– 'Trade before Freedom.' *Le Monde Diplomatique* (November 1999): 1–2.
Gertler, Michael E. 'The Social Economy of Agricultural Sustainability.' In David A. Hay and Gurcharn S. Basran (eds.), *Rural Sociology in Canada*. Toronto: Oxford University Press, 1992.
Geuss, Raymond. *The Idea of a Critical Theory: Habermas and the Frankfurt School.* Cambridge: Cambridge University Press, 1981.
Gill, Stephen. 'Reflections on Global Order and Sociohistorical Time.' *Alternatives* 16, no. 3 (summer 1991): 275–314.
Globalism Project, The Parkland Institute, University of Alberta, Edmonton, 2001. www.ualberta.ca/~parkland/mcri.html.
Godínez, Victor M. 'Una crónica sobre la economía mundial en el cambio de siglo.' In José Luis León (ed.), *El nuevo sistema internacional: Una visión desde México.* Mexico: SRE and FCE, 1999.
Goldsmith, E. 'Can the Environment Survive the Global Economy?' *Ecologist* 27, no. 6 (1997): 242–8.
Gonick, Cy. 'A Democratic Socialist Vision for the 21st Century.' *Canadian Dimension* (March-April, 2001): 34–9.
Goodstein, Eban S. *Economics and the Environment.* Englewood Cliffs, NJ: Prentice Hall, 1999.
Gorman, Michael E., Matthew M. Mehalik, and Patricial H. Werhane. *Ethical and Environmental Challenges to Engineering.* Englewood Cliffs. NJ: Prentice Hall, 2000.
Gramsci, Antonio. *Selections from the Prison Notebooks of Antonio Gramsci*, ed. Quintin Hoare and Geoffrey Nowell Smith. New York: International Publishers, 1971.
Green, M.B., and S.P. Meyer. 'An Overview of Commuting in Canada with Special Emphasis on Rural Commuting and Employment.' *Journal of Rural Studies* 13, no. 2 (1997): 163–75.
Gregory, Derek. 'Critical Theory.' In R.J. Johnston, Derek Gregory, Geraldine Pratt, and Michael Watts (eds.), *Dictionary of Human Geography.* 4th ed. Malden, Mass.: Blackwell, 2000. 129–33.
– 'Existentialism.' In R.J. Johnston, D. Gregory, Geraldine Pratt, and Michael Watts (eds.), *Dictionary of Human Geography.* 4th ed., Malden, Mass.: Blackwell, 2000. 242–3.
Habermas, Jürgen. *Knowledge and Human Interests.* Trans. Jeremy J. Shapiro. Boston: Beacon Press, 1978.
– *The Theory of Communicative Action.* Vol. 1. Trans. Thomas McCarthy. Boston: Beacon Press, 1984.

– *The Theory of Communicative Action*, Vol. 2. Trans. Thomas McCarthy. Boston: Beacon Press, 1987.
– *The Philosophical Discourse of Modernity*. Trans., Frederick Lawrence. Cambridge, Mass.: MIT Press, 1992.
– *Postmetaphysical Thinking: Philosophical Essays*. Trans. William Mark Hohengarten. Cambridge, Mass.: MIT Press, 1992.
Hall, Budd L. 'Global Civil Society: Theorizing a Changing World.' *Convergence* 33 nos. 1, 2 (2000): 10–31.
Hardin, Garrett. 'The Tragedy of the Commons.' *Science* 162, no. 3859 (13 December 1968): 1243–8.
Hardoy, Jorge E., Diana Mitlin, and David Satterthwaite. *Environmental Problems in Third World Cities*. London: Earthscan, 1997.
Hart, Maureen. 1998. 'Sustainability.' www.sustainablemeasures.com/ Sustainability/KeyTermSustain.html.
Hart, Mechthild U. *Working and Educating for Life: Feminist and International Perspectives on Adult Education*. New York: Routledge, 1992.
Harvey, David. 'Between Space and Time: Reflections on the Geographical Imagination.' *Annals of the Association of American Geographers* 80, no. 3 (1990): 418–34.
Hayter, Roger. '"The War in the Woods": Post-Fordist Restructuring, Globalization, and the Contested Remapping of British Columbia's Forest Economy.' *Annals of the Association of American Geographers* 93, no. 3 (2003): 706–29.
Held, David. 'Regulating Globalization? The Reinvention of Politics.' *International Sociology* 15, no. 2 (2000): 233–48.
Helvacioglu, Banu. 'Globalization in the Neighbourhood.' *International Sociology* 15, no. 2 (2000): 326–42.
Henderson, Hazel. *Beyond Globalization: Shaping a Sustainable Global Economy*. New Haven, Conn.: Kumarian Press, 1999.
Hessing, Melody. 'Women and Sustainability: Ecofeminist Perspectives.' *Alternatives* 19, no. 4 (1993): 14–21.
Hildyard, Nicholas. 'Liberation Ecology.' In Edward Goldsmith, Martin Khor, Helena Norberg-Hodge, Vandana Shiva, et al. *The Future of Progress: Reflections on Environment and Development*. Devon: Green Books, 1995.
Holub, Renate. *Antonio Gramsci: Beyond Marxism and Postmodernism*. New York: Routledge, 1992.
Hunter, Allen. 'Globalization from Below? Promises and Perils of the New Internationalism.' *Social Policy* 25, no. 4 (1995): 6–13.
Hunter, Colin. 'Sustainable Tourism as an Adaptive Paradigm.' *Annals of Tourism Research* 24, no. 4 (1997): 850–67.
Ikerd, John. 'Destructive Factory Farms Rapidly Displacing Family Farmers.' *CCPA Monitor* 10, no. 6 (2003): 1, 8.

Jackson, Peter. 'Commodity Cultures: The Traffic in Things.' *Transactions of the Institute of British Geographers.* Vol. 24, 1999. 95–108.

Jacob, Steve, Lisa Bourke, and A.E. Luloff. 'Rural Community Stress, Distress, and Well-being in Pennsylvania.' *Journal of Rural Studies* 13, no. 3 (1997): 275–88.

Jacoby, Russell. 'A Brave Old World: Looking Forward to a Nineteenth-Century Utopia.' *Harper's*, December, 2000. 72–80.

Jayasuriya, Sisira. 'Economists on Sustainability.' *Review of Marketing and Agricultural Economics* 60, no. 2 (1992): 231–41.

Johnson, B.J. Review of *Beyond the Amber Waves of Grain: An Examination of Social and Economic Restructuring in the Heartland,* by P.F. Lasley, F.L. Leistritz, L.M. Lobao, and K. Meyer. *Rural Sociology* 61, no. 3 (1996): 530–3.

Johnson, Doyle Paul. 'Security versus Autonomy Motivation in Anthony Giddens' Concept of Agency.' *Journal for the Theory of Social Behaviour* 20, no. 2 (1990): 11–130.

Johnston, Ron. 'Theory.' In R.J. Johnston, D. Gregory, and D.M. Smith (eds.), *Dictionary of Human Geography*, Malden, Mass.: Blackwell, 1994.

– 'Utility Theory.' In R.J. Johnston, D. Gregory, and D.M. Smith, *Dictionary of Human Geography.* Malden, Mass.: Blackwell, 1994. 666.

Jones, R., and M. Tonts. 'Rural Restructuring and Social Sustainability: Some Reflections on the Western Australian Wheatbelt.' *Australian Geographer* 25, no. 2 (1995): 133–40.

Kane, Melinda. 'Sustainability Concepts: From Theory to Practice.' In Köhn, Jörg, John Gowdy, Friedrich Hinterberger, and Jan van der Straaten (eds.), *Sustainability in Question: The Search for a Conceptual Framework.* Northampton, Mass.: Edward Elgar, 1999.

Kaufman, Cynthia. 'The Unforced Force of the More Familiar Argument.' *Philosophy Today* 43, no. 4 (winter 1999): 348–60.

Kemmis, Stephen, and Robin McTaggart. 'Participatory Action Research.' In Norman K. Denzin and Yvonna S. Lincoln (eds.), *Handbook of Qualitative Research.* 2d ed. Thousand Oaks, Calif.; Sage, 2000.

Kerr, Joanna. 'Women's Rights in the Global Economy: Can Feminists Transform Development?' Sixth Annual Hopper Lecture. 27 October, University of Guelph. Guelph, Ont. 1998.

Khor, Martin. 'Development, Trade and the Environment: A Third World Perspective.' In Edward Goldsmith, Martin Khor, Helena Norberg-Hodge, Vandana Shiva, et al., *The Future of Progress: Reflections on Environment and Development.* Devon: Green Books, 1995.

Kidd, A.D., J.P.A. Lamers, P.P. Ficarelli, and V. Hoffmann. 'Privatising Agricultural Extension: Caveat Emptor.' *Journal of Rural Studies* 16 (2000): 95–102.

Kilpatrick, Sue, Ian Falk, and Lesley Harrison. 'Learning in Rural Communities: A Response to Rapid Economic Change.' CRLRA Discussion Paper Series, 1998. ERIC document number ED 444 772.

Kimbrell, Andrew. 'Seven Deadly Myths of Industrial Agriculture.' In Andrew Kimbrell (ed.), *The Fatal Harvest Reader: The Tragedy of Industrial Agriculture.* Washington, DC: Island Press, 2002.

Kingsnorth, Paul. 'The Heads of the Hydra.' *Ecologist* 29, no. 3 (1999): 203–4.

Köhn, Jörg, John Gowdy, Friedrich Hinterberger, and Jan van der Straaten. 'The Imperative of Sustainability: Introduction.' In Jörg Köhn et al. (eds.), *Sustainability in Question: The Search for a Conceptual Framework.* Northampton, Mass.: Edward Elgar, 1999.

Kolko, Joyce. *Restructuring the World Economy.* New York: Pantheon Books, 1988.

Korsgaard, O. 'Internationalization and Globalization.' *Adult Education and Development* 49 (1997): 9–28.

Korten, David C. 'Sustainable Development.' *World Policy Journal* 9, no. 1 (1991–2): 157–90.

– 'A Not So Radical Agenda for a Sustainable Global Future.' *Convergence* 26, no. 2 (1993): 57–66.

– 'Sustainable Livelihoods: Redefining the Global Social Crisis.' In H. Svi Shapiro and David E. Purpel (eds.), *Critical Social Issues in American Education: Transformation in a Postmodern World.* Mahwah, NJ: Lawrence Erlbaum Associates, 1998.

Kristof, N.D. 'As Life for Family Farmers Worsens, the Toughest Wither.' *New York Times.* 2 April 2000. http://www.nytimes.com.

Kumar, Krishan. 'Civil Society.' In Alan Bullock and Stephen Trombley (eds.), *New Fontana Dictionary of Modern Thought.* London: HarperCollins, 1999.

Kumar, Ranjit, Edward W. Manning, and Barbara Murck. *The Challenge of Sustainability.* Don Mills, Ont.: Foundation for International Training, 1993.

Ladson-Billings, Gloria. 'Racialized Discourses and Ethnic Epistemologies.' In Norman K. Denzin and Yvonna S. Lincoln (eds.), *Handbook of Qualitative Research.* 2d ed. Thousand Oaks, Calif.: Sage, 2000.

Lauzon, A.C. 'Exploring the Foundations of an Adult Education for Sustainable Development.' EdD thesis, Ontario Institute for Studies in Education, University of Toronto, 1995.

Lauzon, A.C., and L.O. Hagglund. 'From the Ground Up: Health Care Restructuring and the Health of Rural Communities.' A report prepared for the SRC Research Program, Ontario Ministry of Agriculture, Food and Rural Affairs. October, 1998.

Lauzon, A.C., and D. Leahy. 'Educational Reform and the Rural Community:
An Ontario Perspective.' A report prepared for the SRC Research Program,
Ontario Ministry of Agriculture, Food and Rural Affairs (Project 023450),
2000.

Laxer, Gordon. 'Social Solidarity, Democracy and Global Capitalism.' *Canadian
Review of Sociology and Anthropology* 32, no. 3 (1995): 287–313.

– 'Radical Transformative Nationalisms Confront the US Empire.' *Current
Sociology* 51, no. 2 (2003): 133–52.

Leach, B., and A. Winson. 'Bringing Globalization Down to Earth: Restructuring and Labour in Rural Communities.' *Canadian Review of Sociology and
Anthropology* 32, no. 3 (1995): 341–63.

Lee, Kai N. 'Greed, Scale Mismatch, and Learning.' *Ecological Applications* 3,
no. 4 (1993): 560–4.

Levis, Nicholas. Introduction to 'Global Circus: Narratives of Globalization,'
Special issue, *International Journal of Political Economy* 26, no. 3 (1996).

Liepins, Ruth. '*Women in Agriculture*: Advocates for a Gendered Sustainable
Agriculture.' *Australian Geographer* 26, no. 2 (1995): 118–26.

Lind, C. 'Is the Rural Population of Saskatchewan a Sustainable Species?'
Moderator's Consultation on Faith and the Economy. Series 2. Paper 3.
12 July 1999. http://www.faith-and-the-economy.org.

Lipsey, Richard G., Christopher T.S. Ragan, and Paul N. Courant. *Microeconomics*. Don Mills, Ont.: Addison-Wesley, 1997.

Lipson, Leslie. *The Great Issues of Politics*. Englewood Cliffs, NJ: Prentice Hall,
1981.

Little, Jo, and Patricia Austin. 'Women and the Rural Idyll.' *Journal of Rural
Studies* 12, no. 2 (1996): 101–11.

Livingstone, David W. *Class Ideologies and Educational Futures*. London: Falmer
Press, 1983.

Lobao, L.M. Industrialized Farming and Its Relationship to Community Well-
Being: Report Prepared for the State of South Dakota, Office of the Attorney
General. Expert testimony for the United States District Court, District of
South Dakota, Central Division, 2001.

Lobao, L.M., and M.D. Schulman. 'Farming Patterns, Rural Restructuring, and
Poverty: A Comparative Regional Analysis.' *Rural Sociology* 56, no. 4 (1991):
565–602.

Lohmann, Larry. 'Whose Common Future?' *Ecologist* 20, no. 3 (1990): 82–4.

Long, Veronica H., and Sara L. Kindon. 'Gender and Tourism Development in
Balinese Villages.' In M. Thea Sinclair (ed.), *Gender, Work and Tourism*. New
York: Routledge, 1997.

Lorenz, F.O., R.D. Conger, R.B. Montague, and K.A.S. Wickrama. 'Economic

Conditions, Spouse Support, and Psychological Distress of Rural Husbands and Wives.' *Rural Sociology* 58, no. 2 (1993): 247–68.

Lynch, C. 'Social Movements and the Problem of Globalization.' *Alternatives* 23, (1998): 149–73.

Lyson, T.A., and C.C. Geisler. 'Toward a Second Agricultural Divide: The Restructuring of American Agriculture.' *Sociologia Ruralis* 32, nos. 2, 3 (1992): 248–63.

Mackenzie, Suzanne, and Glen Norcliffe. 'Restructuring in the Canadian Newsprint Industry.' *Canadian Geographer* 41, no. 1 (1997): 2–6.

Marsden, Terry. 'Restructuring Rurality: From Order to Disorder in Agrarian Political Economy.' *Sociologia Ruralis* 29, nos. 3, 4 (1989): 312–17.

– 'Exploring a Rural Sociology for the Fordist Transition.' *Sociologia Ruralis* 32, nos. 2, 3 (1992): 209–30.

Marsden, Terry, Philip Lowe, and Sarah Whatmore, eds. *Rural Restructuring: Global Processes and Their Responses.* London: David Fulton, 1990.

Marshall, Judith. 'Globalization from Below: The Trade Union Connections.' In Shirley Walters (ed.), *Globalization, Adult Education and Training: Impacts and Issues.* Toronto: ICAE/Zed Books, 1997.

Martinez, Elizabeth, and Arnoldo Garcia. 'What Is "Neo-Liberalism"?' Corporate Watch: Globalization and Corporate Rule. (2000). http://www.corpwatch.org/trac/corner/glob/neolib.html.

Mayo, Peter. *Gramsci, Freire and Adult Education: Possibilities for Transformative Action.* New York: Zed Books, 1999.

Mazur, J. 'Labor's New Internationalism.' *Foreign Affairs* (January/February, 2000): 79–93.

McCarthy, T., trans. 'Translator's Introduction.' In Jürgen Habermas, *The Theory of Communicative Action.* Vol. 1. Boston: Beacon Press, 1984.

McHattie, Bryon. 'Resistance of Farmers in India to GMOs.' Paper presented at the 'Participatory Research and Community Activism in India' Rural Extension Studies Research Conference, University of Guelph. Guelph, Ont. 14 June 2000.

McLaughlin, D.K., E.L. Gardner, and D.T. Lichter. 'Economic Restructuring and Changing Prevalence of Female-Headed Families in America.' *Rural Sociology* 64, no. 3 (1999): 394–416.

McMichael, P. 'Globalization: Myths and Realities.' *Rural Sociology* 61, no. 1 (1996): 25–55.

McMurtry, John. 'Education and the Market Model.' *Journal of Philosophy of Education* 25, no. 2 (1991): 209–17.

– *Unequal Freedoms: The Global Market as an Ethical System.* Toronto: Garamond, 1998.

– *The Cancer Stage of Capitalism.* London: Pluto Press, 1999.
– 'The Lifeground, the Civil Commons and Global Development.' Paper presented at the annual meeting of the Canadian Association for Studies in International Development, Congress of the Social Sciences and Humanities. Sherbrooke, Quebec, 7 June, 1999.
– 'Caging the Poor: The Case against the Prison System.' In W. Gordon West and Ruth Morris (eds.), *The Case for Penal Abolition.* Toronto: Canadian Scholars' Press, 2000.
– Seeing Through the Corporate Agenda: Education. Life-Value and the Global Economy.' Paper presented at the Queen's University Faculty of Education Colloquium 2000, Life and School: Education, Values and the Global Economy. Kingston, Ont., 31 March, 2000.
– 'The Life-Ground, the Civil Commons and the Corporate Male Gang.' Special issue of *Canadian Journal of Development Studies* 22 (2001): 819–54.
– *Value Wars.* London: Pluto Press, 2002.
Meadows, Donella H., Dennis L. Meadows, Jørgen Randers, and William W. Behrens III. *The Limits to Growth: A Report for The Club of Rome's Project on the Predicament of Mankind.* New York: Universe Books, 1972.
Mesarovic, Mihajlo, and Eduard Pestel. *Mankind at the Turning Point: The Second Report to the Club of Rome.* New York: E.P. Dutton and Reader's Digest Press, 1974.
Meyer, John W. 'Globalization: Sources and Effects on National States and Societies.' *International Sociology* 15, no. 2 (June 2000): 233–48.
Mies, Maria, and Veronica Bennholdt-Thomsen. *The Subsistence Perspective: Beyond the Globalised Economy.* Trans. Patrick Camiller, Maria Mies, and Gerd Weih. New York: Zed Books, 1999.
Mies, Maria, and Vandana Shiva. *Ecofeminism.* Halifax/London: Fernwood Publications/Zed Books, 1993.
Milbrath, Lester W. *Envisioning a Sustainable Society: Learning Our Way Out.* Albany: State University of New York Press, 1989.
Miles, Angela. 'Learning from the Women's Movement in the Neo-Liberal Period.' In Sue M. Scott, Bruce Spencer, and Alan M. Thomas (eds.), *Learning for Life: Canadian Readings in Adult Education.* Toronto: Thompson Educational Publishing, 1998.
Mitchell, C.J.A. 'Entrepreneurialism, Commodification and Creative Destruction: A Model of Post-Modern Community Development.' *Journal of Rural Studies* 14, no. 3 (1998): 273–86.
Mojab, Shahrzad. 'The Feminist Project in Cyberspace and Civil Society.' *Convergence* 33 nos. 1, 2 (2000): 106–19.
Monbiot, George. 'The Ethics of Genetics.' *Guardian* (29 June 2000).
– 'Freedom Through Regulation.' *Guardian Weekly* (3–9 May 2001): 21.

– 'Raising the Temperature.' *Guardian Weekly* (26 July – 1 August 2001): 13.

Motchane, Jean-Loup. 'WHO's Responsible?' *Le Monde Diplomatique* (July 2002). 11.

Mowforth, M., and I. Munt. *Tourism and Sustainability: New Tourism in the Third World.* New York: Routledge, 1998.

Murray, M., and L. Dunn. 'Capacity Building for Rural Development in the United States.' *Journal of Rural Studies* 11, no. 1 (1995): 89–97.

Nader, Ralph. 'Stop Americanizing Medicare.' *CCPA Monitor* (February 1996): 17.

Nassauer, Joan Iverson. 'Agricultural Landscapes in Harmony with Nature.' In Andrew Kimbrell (ed.), *The Fatal Harvest Reader: The Tragedy of Industrial Agriculture.* Washington, DC: Island Press, 2002.

Nelson, M.K. 'Economic Restructuring, Gender, and Informal Work: A Case Study of a Rural Economy.' *Rural Sociology* 64, no. 1 (1999): 18–43.

Nielsen, Kai. 'Are Nation-States Obsolete? The Challenge of Globalization.' Paper presented at the Society for Socialist Studies, Congress of the Social Sciences and Humanities. Quebec City, May 2001.

Nikiforuk, Andrew. 'Sustainable Rhetoric.' *Harrowsmith*, vol. 15:3, no. 93 (1990): 14, 16.

Norberg-Hodge, Helena. 'Turning the Globalisation Tide.' *Ecologist* 29, no. 3, (May/June 1999): 200–2, 208.

Norcliffe, Glen. 'Regional Labour Market Adjustments in a Period of Structural Transformation: An Assessment of the Canadian Case.' *Canadian Geographer* 38, no. 1 (1993): 2–17.

– 'Restructuring in the Canadian Newsprint Industry.' *Canadian Geographer* 41, no. 1 (1997): 2–6.

Norgaard, Richard B. 'Sustainable Development: A Co-Evolutionary View.' *Futures* 20, no. 6 (1988): 606–20.

North Carolina State University. 'Agriculture and Rural Viability.' ERIC monograph No. ED307081, 1988.

Nozick, M. *No Place Like Home: Building Sustainable Communities.* Ottawa: Canadian Council on Social Development, 1992.

OMAFRA. '2001–2002 Business Plan.' Ministry of Agriculture, Food and Rural Affairs, 2001. http://www.gov.on.ca.

O'Riordan, Timothy. 'What Does Sustainability Really Mean?' Paper presented at the World Commission on Environment and Development Conference on Sustainable Development in an Industrial Economy, São Paulo, Brazil. November, 1985.

– 'Politics of Sustainability.' In R. Kerry Turner (ed.), *Sustainable Environmental Management: Principles and Practice.* New York: Belhaven Press, 1988.

– 'The Politics of Sustainability.' In R. Kerry Turner (ed.), *Sustainable Environmental Economics and Management: Principles and Practice.* New York: Belhaven Press, 1993.

Orr, David W. *Ecological Literacy: Education and the Transition to a Postmodern World.* Albany: State University of New York Press, 1992.

– 'Ecological Literacy.' In Carlos Hernandez and Rashmi Mayur (eds.), *Pedagogy of the Earth: Education for a Sustainable Future.* Mumbai: International Institute for Sustainable Future, 2000.

O'Sullivan, Edmund. *Transformative Learning: Educational Vision for the 21st Century.* Toronto and London: University of Toronto Press and Zed Books, 1999.

Pacione, M. 'Local Exchange Trading Systems – A Rural Response to the Globalization of Capitalism?' *Journal of Rural Studies* 13, no. 4 (1997): 415–27.

Padavic, I. 'Agricultural Restructuring and the Spatial Dynamics of U.S. Women's Employment in the 1970s.' *Rural Sociology* 58, no. 2 (1993): 210–32.

Palast, Gregory. 'The Ugliness of Pleasantville USA.' *Observer* (22 October 2000). www.gregpalast.com.

– 'The Globalizer Who Came in from the Cold.' *The Observer* (10 October 2001). www.gregpalast.com.

Pan, Philip P. 'China's New Laborers Forced to Work Till They Drop.' *Guardian Weekly* (23–29 May 2002): 37.

Parker, G. 'ELMs Disease: Stewardship, Corporatism and Citizenship in the English Countryside.' *Journal of Rural Studies* 12, no. 4 (1996): 399–411.

Pass, Christopher, Bryan Lowes, Leslie Davis, and Sidney J. Kronish. *HarperCollins Dictionary of Economics.* New York: Harper Perennial, 1991.

Pawson, E., and G. Scott. 'The Regional Consequences of Economic Restructuring: The West Coast, New Zealand (1984–1991).' *Journal of Rural Studies* 8, no. 4 (1992): 373–386.

Peacock, Kent A. 'Sustainability as Symbiosis: Why We Can't Be the Forehead Mites of Gaia.' *Alternatives* 21, no. 4 (1995): 16–22.

– 'Symbiosis and the Ecological Role of Philosophy.' *Dialogue* 38 (1999): 699–717.

– 'Sustainability as a Manifestation of the Second Law of Thermodynamics.' Paper presented to the Department of Philosophy, University of Guelph, Guelph. Ont., 20 March 2000.

Pezzey, John. 'Definitions of Sustainability.' CEED Discussion Paper No. 9. UK Centre for Economic and Environmental Development, 1989.

Pinder, K. 'The Changing Role of Ontario's Ministry of Agriculture, Food and Rural Affairs.' In J.M. Bryden (ed.), *Toward Sustainable Rural Communities: The*

Guelph Seminar Series. Guelph, Ont.: University School of Rural Planning and Development, University of Guelph (1994): 177–9.

Pratt, Geraldine. 2000. 'Participatory Action Research.' In R.J. Johnston, Derek Gregory, Geraldine Pratt, and Michael Watts (eds.), *Dictionary of Human Geography.* 4th ed., Malden, Mass.: Blackwell, 574.

Pretty, Jules N. *Regenerating Agriculture: Policies and Practice for Sustainability and Self-Reliance.* Washington, DC: Joseph Henry Press, 1995.

Prugh, Thomas. *Natural Capital and Human Economic Survival.* Solomons, Md.: International Society for Ecological Economics: ISEE Press, 1995.

Prugh, Thomas, Robert Costanza, and Herman Daly. *The Local Politics of Global Sustainability.* Washington, DC: Island Press, 2000.

Qualman, Darrin. 'The Fight for the Family Farm.' *Quarterly Review,* Canadian Centre for Policy Alternatives – Manitoba (winter 2000).

– 'Corporate Hog Farming: The View from the Family Farm.' In Roger Epp and Dave Whitson (eds.), *Writing Off the Rural West: Globalization, Governments and the Transformation of Rural Communities.* Edmonton: University of Alberta Press and the Parkland Institute, 2001.

Ramsey, Doug, and John C. Everitt. 'Post-Crow Farming in Manitoba: An Analysis of the Wheat and Hog Sectors.' In Roger Epp and Dave Whitson (eds.), *Writing Off the Rural West: Globalization, Governments, and the Transformation of Rural Communities.* Edmonton: University of Alberta Press and the Parkland Institute, 2001.

Ratner, R.S. 'Many Davids, One Goliath.' In William K. Carroll (ed.), *Organizing Dissent: Contemporary Social Movements in Theory and Practice.* Toronto: Garamond, 1997.

Redclift, Michael. 'The Multiple Dimensions of Sustainable Development.' *Geography* 76, no. 330 (January 1991): 36–42.

– 'Sustainable Development: Needs, Values, Rights.' *Environmental Values* 2 (1993): 3–20.

– 'Sustainability and Sociology: Northern Preoccupations.' In Egon Becker and Thomas Jahn (eds.), *Sustainability and the Social Sciences: A Cross-Disciplinary Approach to Integrating Environmental Considerations into Theoretical Reorientation.* New York: Zed Books, 1999.

– *Sustainability: Life Chances and Livelihoods.* New York: Routledge, 2000.

Reed, Maureen. '"Jobs Talk": Retreating From the Social Sustainability of Forestry Communities.' *Forestry Chronicle* 75, no. 5 (1999): 755–63.

– 'Endangered Forests and Endangered Communities.' Proceedings of the 'Nature and Culture of Forests: Implications of Diversity for Sustainability, Trade and Certification,' University of British Columbia, Vancouver, 10–12 May 2001.

Rees, William E. 'Integrating Economy/Ecology: Toward a Role for Environ-
    mental Assessment in Sustainable Development.' UBC Planning Papers.
    Discussion Paper No. 13, School of Community and Regional Planning,
    University of British Columbia, Vancouver, 1988.
– 'The Ecology of Sustainable Development.' *Ecologist* 20, no. 1 (January–
    February 1990): 18–23.
– 'More Jobs, Less Damage: A Framework for Sustainability, Growth and Em-
    ployment.' *Alternatives* 21, no. 4 (1995): 24–30.
– 'Globalization and Sustainability: Conflict or Convergence?' *Bulletin of Science,
    Technology and Society* 22, no. 4 (2002): 249–68.
Rees, William E., and Mark Roseland. 'Sustainable Communities: Planning for
    the 21st Century.' *Plan Canada* 31, no. 3 (1991): 15–26.
Reid, David. *Sustainable Development: An Introductory Guide*. London: Earthscan,
    1995.
Reid, Donald G., Heather Mair, and James Taylor. 'Community Participation in
    Rural Tourism Development.' *World Leisure* no. 2 (2000): 20–7.
Richardson, Nigel. 'What Is a "Sustainable City"?' *Plan Canada* (September 1996):
    34–8.
Rifkin, Jeremy. *The End of Work: The Decline of the Global Labor Force and the Dawn of
    the Post-market Era*. New York: G.P. Putnam's Sons, 1995.
Rivera, W.M. 'Impacts of Extension Privatization.' *Journal of Extension* 31, no. 3
    (1993). http://www.joe.org/joe/1993fall/intl1.html.
Robinson, John, George Francis, Russel Legge, and Sally Lerner. 'Defining a
    Sustainable Society: Values, Principles and Definitions.' *Alternatives* 17, no. 2
    (1990): 36–46.
Roddick, Anita. 'WTO's Charm Offensive.' *Guardian Weekly* (26 July–1 August
    2001): 15.
Röling, Niels. 'An Idea Called Knowledge System.' Presentation to the Rural
    Extension Studies Colloquium Series, University of Guelph. Guelph, Ont.,
    23 October 2000.
– 'Gateway to the Global Garden: Beta/Gamma Science for Dealing with
    Ecological Rationality.' Eighth Annual Hopper Lecture. University of Guelph.
    Guelph, Ont., 24 October, 2000.
Röling, Niels, and Wagemakers, M. *Facilitating Sustainable Agriculture: Participa-
    tory Learning and Adaptive Management in Times of Environmental Uncertainty*.
    Cambridge: Cambridge University Press, 1998.
ROMA (Rural Ontario Municipalities Association). 'Gateways to Change for
    Rural Ontario: Fairness and Equity.' Brief to the Government of the Province
    of Ontario, Ottawa, 1997.
Rosen, Walter. 'Sustainability.' In Alan Bullock and Stephen Trombley (eds.),
    New Fontana Dictionary of Modern Thought, London: HarperCollins, 1999.

Sachs, Ignacy. 'Social Sustainability and Whole Development: Exploring the Dimensions of Sustainable Development.' In Egon Becker and Thomas Jahn (eds.), *Sustainability and the Social Sciences: A Cross-Disciplinary Approach to Integrating Environmental Considerations into Theoretical Reorientation*, New York: Zed Books, 2000.

Sachs, Wolfgang. *Planet Dialectics: Explorations in Environment and Development.* Halifax: Fernwood, 1999.

Salamon, Sonya, and Jane B. Tornatore. 'Territory Contested through Property in a Midwestern Post-Agricultural Community.' *Rural Sociology* 59, no. 4 (1994): 636–54.

Salutin, Rick. 'Walkerton and the Great Transformation.' *Globe and Mail*, 9 June 2000, A15.

Sanders, Richard. 'GATS: The End of Democracy?' *Australian Financial Review* (15 June 2001): 6.

Saul, John Ralston. 'The Collapse of Globalism and the Rebirth of Nationalism.' *Harper's*. March 2004, 33–43.

Schmukler, Sergio L., and Pablo Zoido-Lobatón. 'Financial Globalization: Opportunities and Challenges for Developing Countries,' 2001. http://econ.worldbank.org/prr/doc.php?sp=2477&type=5&id=2839.

Scott, Kathryn, Julie Park, and Chris Cocklin. 'From "Sustainable Rural Communities" to "Social Sustainability": Giving Voice to Diversity in Mangakahia Valley, New Zealand.' *Journal of Rural Studies* 16 (2000): 433–46.

Sewell, J. 'Seminar 2: Opening Remarks.' In T. Fuller and R. Brenner (eds.), *Towards a Sustainable Community: The 1996 Guelph Seminar Series on Sustainability*. Guelph, Ont.: The Guelph Round Table on the Environment and Economy, 1998.

Shearman, Richard. 'The Meaning and Ethics of Sustainability.' *Environmental Management* 14, no. 1 (1990): 1–8.

Shiva, Vandana. 'Resources.' In Wolfgang Sachs (ed.), *The Development Dictionary: A Guide to Knowledge as Power*. Atlantic Highlands, NJ: Zed Books, 1992.

– 'Economic Globalization, Ecological Feminism, and Sustainable Development.' *Canadian Woman Studies* 17, no. 2 (1997): 22–7.

– 'Ecological Balance in an Era of Globalization.' In Nicholas Low (ed.), *Global Ethics and Environment*. New York: Routledge, 1999.

– 'Sustainable Agriculture Must Replace Global Agribusiness.' *CCPA Monitor* (July 1999): 28–9.

Siebenhüner, Bernd. '*Homo sustinens* – Towards a New Conception of Humans for the Science of Sustainability.' *Ecological Economics* 32 (2000): 15–25.

Silva, Eduardo. 'The Politics of Sustainable Development: Native Forest Policy in Chile, Venezuela, Costa Rica and Mexico.' *Journal of Latin American Studies* 29 (1997): 457–93.

Silver, Robert. 'Drive to Globalization Creating a Crisis for Nation-States.' *CCPA Monitor* (June 2002): 30–2.

Simpson, J.A., and E.S.C. Weiner. *Oxford English Dictionary*. 2d ed. Oxford: Clarendon Press, 1989.

Skinner, E. Benjamin. 'How Should the Left Respond to Globalization?' *Dissent* (winter 2001): 9–16.

Sklair, Leslie. 'Social Movements for Global Capitalism: The Transnational Capitalist Class in Action.' *Review of International Political Economy* 4, no. 3 (1997): 514–38.

Smailes, P.J. 'Sustainable Rural Systems: Introduction to a Theme.' *Australian Geographer* 26, no. 2 (1995): 101–3.

– 'Socio-economic Change and Rural Morale in South Australia, 1982–1993.' *Journal of Rural Studies* 13, no. 1 (1997): 19–42.

Solomon, Lawrence. 'Coast-to-Coast Subsidies Trap Rural Canada.' *Financial Post* (19 June 2001), C15.

Soros, George. 'The Capitalist Threat.' *Atlantic Monthly* (February 1997): 45–58.

Sowell, Thomas. *Say's Law: An Historical Analysis*. Princeton: Princeton University Press, 1972.

Stone, Priscilla M, Angelique Haugerud, and Peter D. Little. 'Commodities and Globalization: Anthropological Perspectives.' In Angelique Haugerud, M. Priscilla Stone, and Peter D. Little (eds.), *Commodities and Globalization: Anthropological Perspectives*. New York: Rowman and Littlefield, 2000.

Style, Sophie. 'Gustavo Esteva.' *Z Magazine*. May 2001; 19–24.

Sussman, Gerald. *Communication, Technology and Politics in the Information Age*. Thousand Oaks, Calif.: Sage Publications, 1997.

Suzuki, David. 'Corporate Agriculture: The Hollow Men and Alternative Agriculture: Food for Life.' *The Nature of Things*. CBC Documentaries, 2004. www.cbc.ca/natureofthings/show_agriculture.html.

Swaim, P. 'Adapting to Economic Change: The Case of Displaced Workers.' In L.J. Beaulieu and D. Mulkey (eds.), *Investing in People: The Human Capital Needs of Rural America*. Boulder, Colo.: Westview Press, 1995. 213–34.

Talbot, Lee M. 'A World Conservation Strategy.' *Journal of the Royal Society of the Arts* (July 1980): 493–510.

Therborn, Göran. 'Introduction: From the Universal to the Global.' *International Sociology* 15, no. 2 (2000): 149–50.

– 'Globalizations: Dimensions, Historical Waves, Regional Effects, Normative Governance.' *International Sociology* 15, no. 2 (June 2000): 151–79.

Thrift, Nigel. 'Commodification.' In R.J. Johnston, D. Gregory, and D.M. Smith (eds.), *Dictionary of Human Geography*. 3d ed. Malden, Mass.: Blackwell, 1994.

– 'Geography of Consumption.' In R.J. Johnston, Derek Gregory, Geraldine

Pratt, and Michael Watts (eds.), *Dictionary of Human Geography*. 4th ed. Malden, Mass.: Blackwell, 2000.

Toman, Michael A. 'The Difficulty in Defining Sustainability.' In Joel Darmstadter (ed.), *Global Development and the Environment: Perspectives on Sustainability*. Washington, DC: Resources for the Future, 1992.

Torjman, Sherri. 'Education and the Public Good.' Caledon Institute of Social Policy, Communities and Schools Series. April, 2000. http://www.caledoninst.org.

Troughton, Michael J. 'Conflict or Sustainability: Contrasts and Commonalities Between Global Rural Systems.' *Geography Research Forum* 13 (1993): 1–11.

Turner, R. Kerry (ed.). *Sustainable Environmental Management: Principles and Practice*. Boulder, Colo.: Westview Press, 1988.

Von Kotze, Astrid. 'Monologues or Dialogues? Missed Learning Opportunities in Participatory Rural Appraisal.' *Convergence* 31, no. 4 (1998): 47–55.

Wachtel, Paul L. *The Poverty of Affluence: A Psychological Portrait of the American Way of Life*. Philadelphia: New Society, 1989.

Wallerstein, Immanuel. 'Globalization or the Age of Transition? A Long-term View of the Trajectory of the World-System.' *International Sociology* 15, no. 2 (2000): 249–65.

Waltner-Toews, D. 'Mad Cows and Bad Berries.' *Alternatives Journal* 25, no. 1 (1999): 39–44.

Ward, N., P. Lowe, S. Seymour, and J. Clark. 'Rural Restructuring and the Regulation of Farm Pollution.' *Environment and Planning A* 27 (1995): 1193–1211.

Welton, Michael, ed. *In Defense of the Lifeworld*. Albany: State University of New York Press, 1995.

Wiebe, Nettie. 'Afterword: Rewriting the Rural West.' In Roger Epp and Dave Whitson (eds.), *Writing Off the Rural West: Globalization, Governments, and the Transformation of Rural Communities*. Edmonton: University of Alberta Press, 2001.

Williams, Natalia. 'Church Debates Market Economy.' *Toronto Star*. 15 March 1999, B5.

Wilson, M.G., and E. Whitmore. 'The Transnationalization of Popular Movements: Social Policy Making from Below.' *Canadian Journal of Development Studies* 19, no. 1 (1998): 7–36.

Wilson, O.J. 'Rural Restructuring and Agriculture-Rural Economy Linkages: A New Zealand Study.' *Journal of Rural Studies* 11, no. 4 (1995): 417–31.

Wimberly, D.W. *Review of the Global Restructuring of Agro-Food Systems*, by Philip McMichael (ed.). *Rural Sociology* 61, no. 3 (1996): 537–9.

Wimberley, Ronald C. 'Policy Perspectives on Social, Agricultural, and Rural Sustainability.' *Rural Sociology* 58, no. 1 (1993): 1–29.

Winson, Anthony. 'Does Class Consciousness Exist in Rural Communities? The Impact of Restructuring and Plant Shutdowns in Rural Canada.' *Rural Sociology* 63, no. 4 (1997): 429–53.

Woodgate, Graham, and Michael Redclift. 'From a "Sociology of Nature" to Environmental Sociology: Beyond Social Construction.' *Environmental Values* 7, no. 1 (1998): 3–24.

World Bank. 2001. 'Globalization, Growth and Poverty: Building an Inclusive World Economy.' http://econ.worldbank.org/prr/subpage.php?sp=2477.

World Commission on Environment and Development (WCED). *Our Common Future.* New York: Oxford University Press, 1987.

Worster, Donald. 'The Shaky Ground of Sustainability.' In George Sessions (ed.), *Deep Ecology for the Twenty-first Century.* Boston: Shambhala, 1995.

Yanarella, Ernest J., and Richard S. Levine. 'Does Sustainable Development Lead to Sustainability?' *Futures* 24, no. 8 (1992): 759–74.

Index